FORENSIC GEOLOGY

FORENSIC GEOLOGY

Earth Sciences and Criminal Investigation

RAYMOND C. MURRAY and
JOHN C. F. TEDROW

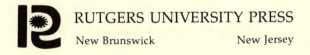

RUTGERS UNIVERSITY PRESS

New Brunswick   New Jersey

Library of Congress Cataloging in Publication Data

Murray, Raymond C
  Forensic geology.

  Includes bibliographies.
  1. Criminal investigation. 2. Chemistry, Forensic.
3. Sediments (Geology)—Analysis. I. Tedrow, J. C. F.,
joint author. II. Title.
HV8073.M86   364.12′01′55   74-18001
ISBN 0-8135-0794-4

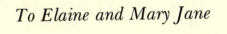

To Elaine and Mary Jane

Contents

Illustrations

FIGURES

TABLES

Preface

Published literature in the field of forensic geology is almost nonexistent. It is the purpose of this book to bring together the available information on the science, outline its basic principles and practices, and encourage the use of new and better techniques in the application of geology to criminalistics.

In this book we address ourselves to three separate and diverse audiences: The *first* are the forensic chemists, attorneys, or law enforcement officers. To these professionals we hope to convey the basic language of geology and soil science and the ideas that should be applicable to their particular problems. The *second* are the professional geologists. For this group we have gathered together the many and diverse applications of geology to criminalistics in the hope that they may find ways in their own work to contribute to the solution of specific problems that may come to their attention. In addition, we hope to stimulate the production of significant new research in the area. The *third* group are the practicing or potential forensic geologists. These persons may be either geologists or soil scientists with training in forensic science. For them the book should offer a background in types of problems and methods. In a sense, it should define a modern professional treatment of soil studies that one would expect in a textbook or handbook of forensic science. It is our feeling that the subject has become sufficiently complex and specialized that such an expanded and separate treatment is needed.

The sample cases cited in the text are all based on fact. Some have been simplified to illustrate a particular point. We have avoided, where possible, giving sufficient information to identify the specific case. The reader who knows of the case, or may have been part of it, may feel that proper credit has not been given. In this we are truly apologetic, but the purpose of this book is basically to offer scientific guidelines, not to compile a casebook of examples to be studied in themselves.

We have not discussed the forensic identification of gems and precious stones and the various types of mine and mineral frauds. These very specialized categories of examination would require a separate book, and demand the highest degree of specialization on the part of the scientist.

Through the years we have discussed these problems and this book with many people. Many others have provided access to information, helped us prepare material, or have given the benefit of their criticism during the writing. We are deeply appreciative to all these people, but in no way do we wish to place on them the burden of responsibility for the contents of the book. The following individuals have been of great assistance to us in the preparation of this book:

Jeffrey Albright, New Jersey State Police

Dr. Robert E. Bergstrom, Illinois Geological Survey

Dr. Peter De Forest, Professor of Criminalistics, John Jay College of Criminal Justice

Ronald Decker, Special Agent, Bureau of Alcohol, Tobacco and Firearms

Kenneth Deffeyes, Princeton University

Harry Eberle, Chief, Piscataway, New Jersey, Police Department

Richard Flach, Virginia Bureau of Forensic Science

William Graves, Centre of Forensic Sciences, Toronto, Ontario, Canada

Paul Jerzak, Lieutenant, Piscataway, New Jersey, Police Department

Dr. Daniel N. Miller, State Geologist, Wyoming

Elmer T. Miller, Special Agent, Federal Bureau of Investigation

Robert Ochs, Assistant Vice-President for Public Safety, Rutgers University

Dr. Richard Saferstein, Chief Chemist, New Jersey State Police
Dr. Arthur A. Socolow, State Geologist, Pennsylvania
L. F. Umholtz, Major, New Jersey State Police
Raymond Vanden Beghe, Sergeant, New Jersey State Police
Dr. Kemble Widmer, State Geologist, New Jersey
Robert Wyzykowski, Captain of Detectives, Rutgers University
    Police

    We are especially indebted to our colleagues at Rutgers
University, particularly those geologists and soil scientists who
have been most helpful with scientific advice.

The *Law Enforcement Bulletin,* published by the Federal Bureau
of Investigation for distribution to law enforcement agencies,
has carried numerous informative articles over the years on the
subject of forensic geology. These have been of great value to us
and several of the cases mentioned have been modified from this
source.

Raymond C. Murray
John C. F. Tedrow

New Brunswick, New Jersey
July 1974

FORENSIC GEOLOGY

1 History of the Science

The geologist has always been a detective. Traditionally he has used his tools and talents for marshaling evidence to locate oil, trace gold or diamonds to their source, or develop the evidence for the drifting of continents. In some cases he has turned these same tools and talents to the development of evidence for the solution of crimes. Examples exist in history and legend where man has combined his powers of observation with past experience to solve such problems using rocks and minerals. The location of the enemy camp, determined from the rocks caught in the horses' hoofs, is a common story. The impression of an unusual patch on the suspect's trousers in moist soil at the scene of a murder provided evidence in a trial in England in 1816.

The ideas for the application of geology by professional geologists to criminalistics began, as did many of the other applications of science to this area, with the writings of Sir Arthur Conan Doyle. Sherlock Holmes pointed the way for many of the ideas and techniques that were later to be discovered by scientists as they attempted to contribute information from their various disciplines to the solution of crimes. The publication of the Sherlock Holmes series between 1887 and 1893 provided the world with ideas that existed only in the mind of Doyle, the physician-author. Those ideas had never actually been used in practice. For example, the venerable Dr. Watson observed of Holmes that he had a knowledge of "Geology—Practical, but limited. Tells at a glance different soils from each other. After walks has shown me splashes upon his trousers,—and told me by their colour and consistence in what part of London he had received them."

Today we would scoff at the idea that Holmes, with the information and techniques available to him in the late nineteenth century, could perform such feats. However, the idea was planted that many soils are unique to small areas on the earth's surface and that man may deliberately or accidentally collect a sample on his person by simply coming in contact with the soil.

In 1893 another author, a criminal investigator and professor of criminology, not a writer of fiction, who may never have heard of Sherlock Holmes, published a practical book outlining ideas for the scientific investigation of crime. Hans Gross, a hard-working Austrian investigator with an interest in the rapidly developing methods of science, compiled the methods currently in use at the time and with remarkable foresight and imagination suggested many potential applications of science to criminal investigation in his classic *Handbuch fur Unter-suchungsrichter* (*Handbook for Examining Magistrates*). The book, originally published in German, was translated into English and appeared under the title *Criminal Investigation*. This re-markable book was reprinted several times and has had a significant impact on the development and use of science in criminal investigation. Gross discussed the applications known at the time in forensic medicine, toxicology, serology and ballistics. Significant to forensic geology, he advocated the employment of the microscopist and mineralogist for the study of "dust, dirt on shoes and spots on cloth." He suggested to the criminal investigator the possibility that contributions could be made by the earth scientist to criminalistics. Most prophetic was his statement, "Dirt on shoes can often tell us more about where the wearer of those shoes had last been than toilsome inquiries." Thus the stage was set by ideas published in fiction and a

Figure 1-1   Professor Dr. Hans Gross, 1847–1915, is generally acknowledged as the founder of scientific criminal investigation. Early in his career he served as legal counsel, State's Attorney, and later in the Appellate Court in Graz, Austria. He championed the exact science of criminal procedure and worked tirelessly in establishing the science of criminology in several universities. Gross was not only concerned with using scientific methods for solving crimes but he also dealt with the underlying causes of crime—the criminal's personality, psychologic changes during confinement, and methods of rehabilitation. (From *Neue Deutsche Biographie Bd.* 7.) *Courtesy of H. Louis*

forward-looking criminalistics handbook for the application of geology and soil science to criminalistics. It is most interesting that the impetus came from ideas in men's minds, not accidentally from actual cases. With the ideas available it was only a matter of time that the applications would be made.

Dr. Georg Popp maintained a laboratory in Frankfurt, Germany. Like many consulting laboratories in the early part of this century, Popp's provided chemical and microscopic services in the area of food studies, mineral water analyses, bacteriology, and many related fields. A chemist by training, he had studied at Marburg, Leipzig, and Heidelberg. Most important, he had the imagination and initiative to search out new applications for the many scientific techniques that were rapidly becoming available. In 1900 a criminal investigator in Frankfurt who had read the Gross book asked him to examine some spots on a suspect's trousers. From this introduction his interest in criminalistics developed and he devoted himself to searching out new methods employing chemical and microscopic techniques. In October 1904 Popp was asked to examine the evidence in a murder case where a seamstress named Eva Disch had been strangled in a bean field with her own scarf. A filthy handkerchief had been left at the scene and the nasal mucus on the handkerchief contained bits of coal, particles of snuff, and, most interesting, grains of minerals, particularly the mineral hornblende. A suspect by the name of Karl Laubach was known to work in a coal-burning gasworks and part-time in a local gravel pit. Popp found coal and mineral grains, particularly the mineral hornblende, under the suspect's fingernails. It was also determined that the suspect used snuff. Examination of soil removed from Laubach's trousers revealed a lower layer in contact with the cloth whose minerals compared with those found in a sample collected from the place where the body of Eva Disch had been found! Encrusted on top of this lower layer a second soil type was found. Examination of the minerals in the upper layer revealed a mineralogy and size of particle, particularly a crushed mica grain, that Popp determined were comparable with soil samples collected from the path that led from the murder scene to the suspect's home. From these data it

Figure 1-2   Dr. Georg Popp, German forensic scientist. In 1904 he developed and presented what is believed to be the first example of evidence in a criminal case using earth materials. *Courtesy of Jürgen Thorwald*

was concluded that the suspect picked up the lower soil layer at the scene of the crime and that this lower, thus earlier material, was covered by splashes of mica-rich mud from the path on his return home. When confronted with the soil evidence Karl Laubach admitted the crime and the Frankfurt newspapers of the day carried headlines such as "The Microscope as Detective." It is impossible to determine from the distance of three-quarters of a century how a forensic geologist or a jury would evaluate the geologic evidence amassed by Popp today. One fact is evident—minerals had been used in an actual case, fulfilling the prophesy of Gross and illustrating a real-life example worthy of the fictional Holmes.

The case that established the value of geologic information occurred in the spring of 1908. Margarethe Filbert was murdered near Rockenhausen in Bavaria. The district attorney, a man by the name of Sohn, in Kaiserslautern, was seeking information on the source of some hairs found in the victim's hands. He was familiar with Gross's book and had filed, for future reference, clippings from the Frankfurt newspaper of 1904 describing Popp's work in the Disch case. District Attorney Sohn located Popp in Frankfurt and asked him to study the hair and other material.

Georg Popp began an intensive study of the available material. He studied the hair and concluded that it came from the victim. Not easily discouraged, he extended his studies to other objects, noting with special interest encrusted soil on the dress shoes of the principal suspect, a local factory worker and farmer named Andreas Schlicher. Schlicher was a person of "low reputations who had previously been suspected of poaching." Following the murder, many of his neighbors had suggested him as a likely suspect. It had been established that Schlicher's wife had cleaned his dress shoes the night before the murder and that he had worn them only on that day. However, he stoutly denied having anything to do with the crime, or having walked on that day in the field where the crime was committed. His trousers had been found in a nearby abandoned castle along with a rifle and ammunition used in poaching. It was established that the ammunition was his. However, he claimed that they had been left at the castle prior to the day of the murder.

Popp collected soil samples from the surrounding area. He studied these, assisted by a geologist by the name of Fischer, and observed that the area immediately surrounding the suspect's home was littered with green goose droppings. The fields of the suspect contained a distinctive soil containing fragments of porphyry, milky quartz, and mica. Root fibers, weathered straw, and leaves were also common. Most interesting was the observation that the scene of the crime had a soil containing decomposed red sandstone, angular quartz, ferruginous clay, and little vegetation. At the castle where the trousers and gun were found, the soil contained coal, abundant brick dust, and broken pieces of cement from the crumbling walls.

Upon examining the dress shoes of the suspect, Popp was impressed with the thickly caked soil on the sole of the shoes in front of the heel. He reasoned that the soil must have accumulated as the suspect walked, on the one day he had worn the shoes. That one day was the day of the murder. In addition, he reasoned that the layers of soil that accumulated on the shoes represented a sequential deposit with the earliest material deposited directly on the leather. Careful removal of the individual layers revealed the following sequence: First a layer of goose droppings directly on the leather followed by grains of red sandstone. A mixture of coal, brick dust, and cement fragments rested on top of the sandstone. In all three layers Popp was able to compare the material on the shoe with the soil from near the suspect's home, the scene of the crime, and the castle. Although Schlicher had claimed he had walked in his own fields, no fragments of porphyry with milky quartz were found on the shoes. The comparison of the soil on the shoes with the scene of the crime and the scene where the trousers were discarded indicated that the suspect had lied and had been at these places on the day of the crime.

Georg Popp made many contributions to forensic science. However, the Margarethe Filbert case established him in the field of forensic geology and set the stage for later studies of soil comparison. In this early case he had established a time sequence of soil accumulation representing the places where a person had walked. Hans Gross had been right. The dirt on the shoes had told more than had been obtained from intensive interrogation.

In 1906 Conan Doyle became involved in an actual criminal case where he applied some of the methods of the fictional Holmes. This was the first of three cases where the writer became the investigator. An English solicitor was accused and convicted of cutting and mutilating animals, specifically horses and cows. After serving three years in prison he was released but not pardoned, despite some evidence that he was actually innocent of the crimes. Doyle became interested in the case. In developing additional evidence he observed that the soil on the convicted man's shoes worn on the day of the last crime was black mud and not the yellow sandy clays found in the field where the pony had been killed. This observation combined with other evidence led to a full pardon for the convicted man.

In France, Edmond Locard, who was a student of Alexandre Lacassagne, one of the early leaders in forensic medicine, read French translations of the *Adventures of Sherlock Holmes* and parts of Gross's book. The fact that the criminal came into contact with bits of dust during the crime and that these bits of dust were often transferred to the criminal intrigued Locard. After many failures to develop a laboratory and an interest in scientific criminalistics, he was finally given, in the summer of 1910, two attic rooms in Lyons and two Sûreté assistants. In these rooms he did remarkable work with identification of particles and developed a reputation for being able to provide information that was useful in investigations.

Emile Gourbin, in 1912, was a bank clerk in Lyons. He came under suspicion of murdering, by strangulation, his girl friend, Marie Latelle. Gourbin was arrested but produced what appeared to be an airtight alibi. Locard went to Gourbin's cell and removed scrapings from under his fingernails. These scrapings contained tissue that might have come from Marie's neck but this was not provable. Locard noticed that the tissue was coated with a pink dust which he identified as rice starch. On the particles he found bismuth, magnesium stearate, zinc oxide, and a reddish iron oxide pigment, Venetian red. Examination of face powder used by Marie revealed that a powder prepared for her by a Lyons druggist was similar in composition. In these days of mass-produced face powder, this evidence would have far less significance. However, in 1912, because of the special preparation, it led to the confession of Gourbin.

In the following years Locard was to study, catalogue, and use in many cases the bits of dust found associated with crimes and suspects. These bits of dust were often minerals or related materials.

In the United States, the small town of Colma, California,

was shocked when, on the night of August 2, 1921, the parish priest, Father Patrick Heslin, was kidnapped. A ransom note was received but no further contact was made and the priest was assumed to have been murdered. In a remarkable bit of genius or luck, Edward Heinrich examined handwriting on the note and announced to the police that the writer "had the hand" of a baker and decorator of cakes. Thus when William Hightower reported to police that he had learned of the location of the body of Father Heslin, they were immediately suspicious that he might know more than he admitted. Hightower was a master baker.

Edward Oscar Heinrich, sometimes known as the "wizard of Berkeley," was already one of the most famous criminalists in the country. His remarkable work with physical evidence in the areas of paint, fibers, ballistics, poisons, hair, and wood had won this hard-working, skillful California chemist a reputation for being able to use physical evidence to assist investigation, and later present the evidence in court. Born in Clintonville, Wisconsin, in 1881, he graduated from the University of California at Berkeley and later became professor of criminology. Despite a somewhat dramatic style and self-assurance, his contributions to forensic science were remarkable.

Heinrich examined the place on the California beach where Hightower indicated the body of Father Heslin would be found. The body was found and the investigation also produced a number of objects of physical evidence such as boards from a tent floor. Heinrich studied grains of sand recovered from Hightower's knife and pronounced them similar to the sand on the beach where the body was found. In Hightower's room a tent was found and the tent contained an abundance of sand which, when studied, confirmed the results from the knife. It appeared that Hightower had kidnapped and murdered Father Heslin and kept his body in the tent on the beach for several days before burying it in the sand. Having done these things, he then reported having received information about the location of the body to the police. Hightower's trial resulted in conviction and he was sentenced to life imprisonment at San Quentin Penitentiary.

In 1925 Heinrich undertook an intriguing case that was to

apply his knowledge of geology. Mrs. Sidney d'Asquith, sometimes known as Mrs. J. J. Loren, had been murdered and her
body dismembered. Parts of the body, including an ear, were
found in a marsh near El Cerrito, California. The rest of the
body could not be found despite an intense search. Heinrich
determined that the grains of sand he found on the ear of the
victim did not come from the black mud of the marsh and
reasoned that the body with the ear attached had been placed
elsewhere. Later the ear with the sand grains from the earlier
location and part of the head had been removed and taken to the
marsh. He studied the sand grains, noting their size and
composition. He also observed that they had what he considered
insufficient salt crystals adhering to them to have been sand
from an ocean beach. There was some salt present and he
deduced that it came from a river or brook at a place where it
entered the ocean. He studied maps with the assumption that he
was looking for the nearest place to the marsh where such
conditions exist. The place he suggested was Bay Farm Island,
twelve miles from the marsh at El Cerrito, and the site of San
Leandro Creek. Despite some doubts, a search was instigated at
Bay Farm Island and the rest of the body was found buried
under the drawbridge. The case has never been solved.
However, the combination of skill, and perhaps luck, which
Heinrich employed introduced forensic geology to the United
States in a most dramatic way.

The Federal Bureau of Investigation Laboratory was one of
the first forensic laboratories in the United States to extensively
use soil and mineral analysis in criminal cases. As early as 1935
the FBI Laboratory was working with soils. In late 1936 the
Matson kidnapping case involved examinations of soil from the
victim's left hand with a view to determining by mineral analysis
where the boy was kept prior to his murder. By early 1939 heavy
mineral separations and mineral identifications were standard
practices in the FBI Laboratory in soil cases.

Today most of the major crime laboratories, both public
and private, throughout the world study soils on a routine basis.
Great differences in the quality of the analyses exist, depending
on staff training, experience, availability of equipment, time,

and the experience of the submitting agency or investigator. Although exact figures are not available, it is safe to estimate that thousands of cases are studied in North America alone each year where geologic material, usually soil, has been collected as part of the routine investigation.

In a recent study, Parker and Peterson (1974) have examined the various kinds of physical evidence used in criminal cases. They found that the following categories of evidence were used in cases involving auto theft. (Those involving a significant contribution from forensic geology are marked with an asterisk.)

1. *Toolmarks:* This category includes all physical evidence where it was evident that one object, serving as a tool, acted on another object creating impressions, friction marks, or striations. A screwdriver, pipe, pry bar, fender of an automobile, or barrel of a gun could all produce tool marks.

2. *Fingerprints and palmprints:* All prints of this nature, latent or visible, are included. Barefoot prints, glove, or other fabric prints would be included in this category also.

3. *Organic, botanical, zoological material and unknown stains:* Cases where matter of organic origin or stains of nonorganic nature were discovered. Excreta, all residues from trees and shrubs, and food items were typical examples.

4. *Glass or plastic fragments:* * The presence of broken or chipped glass or plastic in an area suggesting it was the result of the actions of the responsible person or it might have been transferred to person(s) involved in the offense.

5. *Paint:* Liquid or dried paint in positions where transference would be impossible to persons in that area. Freshly painted locations, cracked and peeling paint on window sills, and automobile collisions are leading examples.

6. *Tracks and impressions:* Includes skid and scuff markings, shoe prints, depressions in soft vegetation or soil, and all other forms of tracking. Conventional tool marks would not be included in this category.

7. *Clothing:* Instances where items of clothing are left, carried, removed or discarded by persons. Individual fiber characteristics are in a separate category.

8. *Wood fragments:* Cases where forces have created fragmenting or splintering in areas where transference was likely. Prying, kicking, and chopping attempts at entry points were the most frequent examples.
9. *Dust:* * All cases where "dust" (all types of surface contamination) was noticeably disturbed by someone.
10. *Cigarettes, matches, related ashes:* Discovery of any of these combustible items which were in such position that their relationship to persons responsible was likely.
11. *Paper in various forms:* There are two basic areas of identification for paper. First, where the paper itself might be traced to its original position or orientation, and second, where external information including latent prints and other contaminating substances might be present on the paper.
12. *Soil:* * The presence of soil or soil-like material in locations where identification or individualization seemed possible.
13. *Fibers, natural or synthetic:* Fibers were often found near sharp corners or edges, or on objects where electrostatic or mechanical forces caused a transfer.
14. *Tools and weapons:* Cases where tools and weapons were found at crime scenes or in automobiles and there was a strong likelihood that they were involved in this or another criminal offense.
15. *Grease and oil:* Any lubricant or fatty substance, often possessing environmental contamination, that was in a position to suggest involvement in the crime.
16. *Documents:* Of such quality that their origin may be traced to a person or instrument. Suicides and robbery notes would be of this type. Also cases where instruments were stolen (check protectors) that could be traced back to a product of that particular instrument, in possession of rightful owner.
17. *Containers:* All bottles, boxes, cans and other containers which might hold residues or material of helpful nature.
18. *Construction and packing material:* All those substances commonly found in construction or packing areas, which do not belong to any of the other classifications.
19. *Metal fragments:* Industrial machining areas, scenes or ob-

jects of collisions, and other scrapings that would probably result in transfers to persons or objects in the vicinity.

20. *Hair:* Any animal or human hair discovered in an environment which could link a person with that particular area.
21. *Blood:* All suspected blood, liquid or dried, animal or human, present in a form to suggest a relation to the offense or persons involved.
22. *Inorganic and mineralogical substances:* * All substances, and otherwise not belonging in another category, that could be classified under one of these headings, and bearing a relationship to the offense or offender.

These types of evidence are listed in decreasing order of their presence in the cases studied. This obviously depends on the availability of a given type of evidence in the case and whether or not the investigator collected that evidence.

References

Block, E. B. 1958. *The wizard of Berkeley.* New York: Coward-McCann, Inc.

Doyle, A. C. 1956. *The complete Sherlock Holmes,* vol. 1. New York: Doubleday and Co., Inc.

Gross, H. 1893. *Handbuch fur untersuchungsrichter.* Munich: N.P.

———. 1962. *Criminal investigation.* Trans. J. Adam and J. Collier Adam, revised by R. L. Jackson. London: Sweet and Maxwell.

Hall, J. C. 1974. *Inside the crime lab.* Englewood Cliffs, N.J.: Prentice-Hall, Inc.

Hormachea, C. R. 1974. *Sourcebook in criminalistics.* Reston, Va.: Reston Publishing Co.

Kind, S., and Overman, M. 1972. *Science against crime.* London: Aldus Books, Ltd.

Locard, E. 1928. Dust and its analysis. *Am. Jour. Police Sci.* 1:177–192.

———. 1930. Analyses of dust traces. *Am. Jour. Police Sci.* 1:276, 401–496.

Thorwald, J. 1967. *Crime and science.* New York: Harcourt, Brace and World, Inc.

2 Earth Materials as Physical Evidence

In this chapter we will discuss the evidencial value of soil and related material.

Before any discussion on the nature of earth materials or soil can begin it is necessary to be clear as to what is meant by the term "soil" in forensic science. The agriculturalist and the gardener generally consider soil to be the upper 6- to 12-inch layer of earth in which plants grow. The earth scientist considers the soil to be mineral and organic material forming on the earth's surface as a result of a whole series of complex processes. Some scientists view the soil largely in context of the origin and nature of the surficial materials and accordingly use such terms as moraine soils, lakebed soils, outwash soils, wind-blown soils, and bedrock soils. The mineralogically oriented scientist may, at times, emphasize rock composition and describe sandstone soils, granite soils, diabase soils, and so on. Engineers commonly view the soil as a construction material and focus their attention on the volume of the unconsolidated material—its texture, binding properties, compaction, porosity, bearing capacity, moisture conditions, and related engineering properties. The engineer may use the word *soil* if the material can be removed with mechanical equipment and *rock* where excavation can be done only with explosives. To the layman the term soil generally has an even broader meaning and, in addition to those described conditions, includes gravel, cinders, fly ash, building materials, tar, sewage and a host of other substances. These various concepts all have merit.

The pedologist or soil scientist is primarily interested in the processes taking place in the soil such as mineral alteration, movement of materials, and biochemical changes. As a result of these interests, he may study only a few carefully selected undisturbed natural sites and after meticulous sampling devote years in detailed characterization of the soils somewhat like a geologist with a favorite kind of rock or field area in which he studies a gamut of geologic properties. Many sites would be rejected for pedologic studies on the basis of their having been disturbed by man.

Soils in recently filled areas—commonly referred to as made land, borrow pits, garbage dumps, and even those in most urban areas would normally be rejected as unsuitable for academic study because of alteration and contamination of the sites. But the forensic geologist, by the nature of his subject, must spend much of his time in sampling such areas because they are the scenes of greatest human activity. His soil samples seldom are collected from undisturbed locations; instead they come from fill areas around the home, the parking lot, the highway shoulder, or the unpaved road itself. So the forensic geologist seldom has a wide selection of sites; the area for sample collection has already been largely determined for him by prior events. In effect, many of the samples used in forensic geology result from a mistake or an accident such as mud on the heel of a shoe or silt filtering into machinery.

In southern Ontario a man was arrested and charged with the beating death of a young girl. The scene of the crime was a construction site adjacent to a newly poured concrete wall. The soil was sand which had been transported to the scene for construction purposes. As such, the sand had received additional mixing during the moving and construction process and was quite distinctive. The glove of the suspect contained sand that was similar to that found at the scene and significantly different in composition and particle size from the area of the suspect's home. This was important because the suspect claimed the soil on the gloves came from his garden.

A shoe may easily collect moist clay through simple contact while the same shoe will gather little if any material from an outcropping of hard granite. The important distinction in a forensic definition of soil thus lies in the fact of sampling of earth material, either accidental or deliberate, rather than in any arbitrary definition developed for some other particular purpose. Soil, for forensic purposes, is earth material that has been collected accidentally or deliberately and has some association with the matter under investigation. In considering this definition of a soil, it is well to bear in mind that the related material found with minerals within a soil may include organic particles, such as parts of plants, and a variety of man-made or foreign particles carried to and incorporated into the soil. Although ease of sampling is important to the definition, it is well to bear in mind that small specks of minerals may be brushed off an otherwise hard rock surface and that the use of explosives or a sledge hammer may turn natural rock or artificial rock such as concrete into easily sampled, small-sized particles.

How Do Natural Soils Form?

For the most part, the earth is made of solid rock. The continents are composed of generally light-colored rocks having a relatively high content of silica and, on the average, lower densities than those rocks found underneath the world's oceans. The ocean bottoms are covered with mud and sands containing a variety of minerals. Underneath this sediment are rocks that have been made from older sediment whose mineral grains have bound together naturally. Beneath these rocks, volcanic lava forms most of the solid foundation of the ocean basins. This volcanic rock is generally dark, relatively low in silica content, and is slightly denser than the rocks we see on the continents.

The solid rocks of the continents are usually covered with soil and are only seen where the soil has been removed, as evidenced in cuts made for highways or railroads, along the bank of a river, or at a sea cliff or mountain in a dry climate. The area where the solid rock is exposed at the surface is referred to as an *outcrop*. The solid rocks are generally covered with unconsolidated, loose material composed for the most part of minerals and rocks. This material would, for our purposes, be considered soil. The thickness of the soil material, that is, the distance from the surface of the earth down to solid rock, varies from place to place from a fraction of a millimeter to hundreds of meters.

Soil material may be formed by nature in one of two ways, *residual* or *transported*. Remember that this loose material is composed of fragments of minerals and rocks which were derived from the breaking up or dissolving of solid rocks of the earth. The first method is through the formation of *residual* soil material, that is, material formed in place. In the formation of residual soil material, solid rock is exposed in outcrops at the earth's surface. This rock is then subjected to the natural processes of weathering which tend to break up and dissolve the rock, turning it into a mass of fragments and removing some of the material in solution. The dissolving of the minerals normally occurs in rain water or ground water. The natural breaking up of the solid rock may be accomplished by a variety of methods. Some of the mechanical methods that are especially effective are: frost-wedging, root-wedging, growth of new minerals, and expansion of minerals. In frost-wedging, water seeps into cracks in the rock and freezes to ice. The ice has greater volume than water, thus the crack is forced open, causing the rock to break into fragments. Tree roots have a similar effect. Both these effects can be observed in the many cracked and shattered concrete paths and driveways. New minerals may crystallize from ground water, especially where the chemicals in the water become concentrated by evaporation. As the new minerals grow within the cracks of the rock, they force the crack open, thus further breaking and shattering the rock. Some minerals such as clays expand when wet. This expansion commonly causes the rock to break and crumble. Chemical processes also affect the rock. Rain water and ground water dissolve some minerals more rapidly than others, thereby leaving holes in rocks and ultimately resulting in the crumbling of the solid rock and the formation of soil. In other cases, minerals such as the feldspars or iron- and magnesium-rich silicate minerals are converted to clay minerals after long exposure to water. This change may cause expansion in the size of the mineral grains, forcing the rock to break up into smaller fragments. The net result is the production of a loose mass of soil material from the upper part of the once solid rock. Some of the fragments may be carried away by wind or water or in solution by water. The remaining soil material is produced directly from the underlying rock, thus it is residual, that is, it is produced in place and left behind.

In the second method, soil material is *transported* from other areas. Here the fragments of minerals are produced elsewhere and are transported to the location where they are found. Nature provides many ways for transporting soil-producing materials. For example, dissolved chemical elements carried in river water may supply the calcium that clams use to produce their shells. The accumulated shells of these and other animals may produce a special material for soil formation. Fragments of rocks and minerals created by weathering of a rock outcrop may be carried away by rivers and be deposited as sand bars, gravel, or accumulations of fine mud (Fig. 2-1). Wind moves vast quantities of fragments, depositing them as sand dunes or dust layers. Waves and currents along the shores of the seas and lakes break up rock and mineral fragments, transport them, and ultimately deposit the particles in the form of beaches or sediment beneath the water of lakes or seas. The force of gravity may cause a landslide which moves tons of rock and mineral debris down a slope and produces a mass of newly transported soil on the land below. Of great importance in the northern latitudes or on the tops and slopes of the higher mountains is the fact that prior to 10,000 years ago and for the previous last million-odd years, our planet was subjected to periodic changes in climate marked by unusually cold-wet periods. During these times, glacial ice periodically formed in northern areas and the high mountains. This ice spread as far south as central New Jersey, Ohio, Illinois, and Kansas, and covered many of the mountain peaks in the Rocky Mountains as far south as New Mexico. The same was true for northern Europe and Asia and the higher elevations of the Alps. Moving glacial ice has tremendous power for grinding up

Brown sand

Gravel

Inclined sand

Sand and gravel
that has fallen from
the beds above

Figure 2-1   Poorly consolidated sands and gravel showing three layers, inclined white sand overlain by gravel overlain by brown sand.

and removing rocks. Rocks picked up by the ice gouge and grind away the underlying solid rock (Fig. 2-2). When the ice melts, the rock debris within the ice may be deposited on the newly exposed ground. This rock and mineral debris is called *till* or glacial drift. Glacial *outwash* may be deposited by rivers flowing away from the melting ice, carrying tremendous amounts of rock and mineral fragments. Winds blowing off the glacier may pick up and carry masses of dust and deposit it over wide areas producing a soil called *loess*. When we examine the soils of the glaciated regions, we realize that much of the material was formed as a direct result of the glaciation.

These processes are most important to the forensic geologist. When we consider that the residual soil material can be developed on any one of the almost unlimited types of solid rock and be modified by a large number of different climates, we come to realize the potential diversity of soil characteristics. Specifically, we are impressed with the widely variable possibilities of rock, mineral, and chemical composition of soils and the closely spaced lateral changes in the composition of soil that can and do occur. We then compound this with the effects of

Figure 2-2   Glacially polished outcrop of slate with unconsolidated material on top. Note the long scratches on outcrop that were made by rocks frozen into the moving glacial ice.

transportation of particles and dissolved material from rocks of innumerable compositional differences and of selective deposition at various places on the earth of materials having different size and mineral composition. Thus it is not surprising that we find a vast, almost unlimited number of variations that exist in the characteristics of soil samples from place to place.

Soil Comparison

Earth materials—soils, rocks, minerals, and fossils—can be, and commonly are used as physical evidence in both criminal and civil matters. The most common use, as with all physical evidence such as fingerprints, glass, paint, metals, blood, tool marks, firearms, explosives, etc., is in the contribution of scientific evidence to help establish guilt or innocence of an individual with respect to a certain criminal act. In addition, study of earth material may provide clues during an investigation which will lead to or help establish responsibility in both criminal and civil matters, or in finding or convicting a suspect. In the latter case, for example, it is sometimes possible to establish with considerable assurance that the soil on the shoes of a suspect compares with that found at the scene of the crime. This should indicate, with a very high degree of confidence, that those shoes were in contact with soil at the scene and thus may contribute to the reconstruction of events. Alternatively, a suspect may claim that the soil on the shoes was picked up at another specific location. If the soil on the shoes does not compare with soil of the claimed site, then a low degree of credibility may be assigned to this particular aspect of the story. In an exemplary case, an elderly woman was mugged and murdered in a Washington, D.C., park some years ago and her body was found under a park bench. Within a short time a suspect was apprehended as a result of a description given by a witness who had seen the person leaving the park on the night of the murder. It was obvious that the suspect had been involved in a struggle and he had soil adhering to his clothing and filling his trouser cuffs. He claimed to have been in a fight in another part of the city and gave the location of the fight. Study of the soils near the park bench and of those collected from the scene of the alleged fight revealed that the soil from the suspect's clothing compared with that near the park bench, and did not compare with samples from the area of the described fight. The comparable similarity with the soil sample from the park area strongly suggested that the suspect had been in contact with the ground in that area and cast strong doubt on his statement that he had not been in the park for years. Furthermore, the lack of similarity between the clothing soil samples and those from the area where he claimed to have been fighting questioned the validity of his alibi.

In another case, the soil dislodged from the fender or frame of an automobile during a hit-and-run accident provided a clue to the area where the car had been driven and thus the possible home or past driving area of the person responsible. In the case of a fatal hit-and-run accident in the upper Midwest, clumps of soil dislodged from the fender of the car as it struck the victim and sped away were shown to contain the characteristic minerals of the Missouri lead-zinc mining district hundreds of miles to the south. This knowledge contributed to the successful search for a suspect. When a suspect was apprehended and soil from under the fenders of his car was studied, it was found to compare with the material collected from the highway at the scene of the crime. Furthermore, it was subsequently shown that he had previously driven through mining areas of Missouri where rocks from the mines are used as road material.

In a third case, rocks were substituted for valuable articles in boxes which were in transit and provided a clue to the place where the switch was made by determining where the rocks originated. When a Canadian liquor store owner opened newly arrived cases of Scotch whisky and prepared to place the bottles on the shelf, he was unpleasantly surprised to find blocks of limestone, each of which was of the same weight as a bottle of whisky, neatly placed in each compartment. From study of the limestone, it was determined that it could not have come from any of the places through which the whisky passed in transit, other than from its point of origin, Great Britain. Further study revealed that the limestone in the boxes compared with limestone from a particular quarry in central England and finally, that the suspect, who worked for the liquor distributor and had immediate access to that quarry, had often been seen taking home many samples of the rock.

The use of earth materials, soils, rocks, minerals, and fossils, as for all physical evidence, has both limitations and advantages. The fundamental limitation lies in the fact that significance of such evidence is determined by probability and statistics. No two physical objects are ever exactly the same in a purely theoretical sense. For example, if we were to take a rock from any outcrop and break it into two pieces, in most cases it would be possible to show, by detailed study, differences between the two pieces. The similarity between the two pieces in most cases would be large and we would be able to say that the two pieces compare and that there is a high probability that one piece was a sample of the other. If the two pieces could be fitted together and individual minerals could be shown to be broken and are lined up when fitted back together, then the probability that they were once part of the same rock would be even greater. In this case we would say that we had shown an individual characteristic and that there was really no doubt of the comparison. We would, however, still be dealing with probability and the value of the determination would largely depend on the competence of the scientist who made the determination and availability of data.

In many cases involving earth materials, the probability becomes so high as to approach that of the individual type of evidence such as fingerprints. For example, in a Canadian rape case the knees of the suspect's trousers contained encrusted soil samples. The sample of the right knee was different from that collected from the left knee. In examining the crime scene, two knee impressions were found in the soil corresponding to a right and left knee. Samples taken from these two knee impressions were different. The soil sample collected from the left knee impression compared with that removed from the left trouser knee of the suspect as did the right knee impression and the right trouser knee. A major change in soil type occurred between the two knee impressions, indicating that a contact between two rock or soil types was located at that place.

In general, the usefulness of most types of physical evidence, recognizing that probability and chance are most important, depends upon the number of significant variations that exist in the material and can be easily observed or measured. Specifically, how many different kinds of classes can exist and how widespread is a single class or kind? The value of soils, rock, minerals, and fossils lies in the fact that nature has provided us with a large number of variations and possibilities. When considered in this way, it can be said with some confidence that earth materials offer many opportunities for significant use as physical evidence. When we consider the opportunities based on number of variations, earth materials would rank higher than almost all other forms of physical evidence, excluding such pattern evidence as fingerprints or some firearms and tool-mark comparisons. In considering such a statement, we must immediately recognize three obvious limitations: First, soil evidence must have been present and collected by the investigator. This, in part, means that the investigator must be familiar with the possibilities of soils as evidence and how they are collected and treated. Although the number of variations in blood type demonstrable in dried blood stains may be less than that of soils, blood is easily observed, commonly collected, and often present in certain kinds of crime. The second limitation is that the methods of comparison must be valid, performed by an expert and be in sufficient detail to establish a high degree of confidence in the meaning and usefulness of the comparison. For an undried bulk sample, if only colors of soil were compared by an untrained eye, the comparison of soils would have far less validity than would expert comparison of paint by color and chemical analysis. The third limitation is that the earth material may be picked up by a person over a period of time and thus a comparison with samples from a single crime scene may be meaningless. For example, soil from the floorboard of a vehicle may represent the accumulation of years of dirty shoes or may have resulted from one set of dirty shoes at one time. The simple comparison of soil samples from a crime scene with the collected material from a floorboard is roughly analogous to the attempted comparison of the fibers of a jacket found at the scene of a crime with the floor sweepings of a clothing store. Fibers from the coat may compare with some of the fibers from the clothing store floor, but a simple comparison between the two samples is usually impossible. The same is true with the soil from the floorboard of the vehicle. While it is sometimes possible to recognize distinctive and unusual minerals and rocks from a crime scene and compare them with minerals and rocks removed from the floorboard of a vehicle with a high degree of confidence, an overall or superficial comparison of the two samples is meaningless.

The advantage of soils, rocks, minerals, and fossils or any physical evidence lies in the scientific objectivity of the analysis and testimony of the expert. This has been discussed by many authors writing on the general subject of evidence. Most geologists have experienced the sometimes questionable value of statements made by eyewitnesses in their daily work. Stories such as that of the landowner who swore he saw the oil flow from a wildcat well on his property before it was abandoned, only to have it refuted by the oil company as being dry on the basis of expert analysis, thereby destroying his hopes for wealth, are common. There is also the case of the man who rushed into the office of a coastal New Jersey police department with an object which he claimed landed at his feet in a flaming streak from outer space. It was later shown to be a wave-worn piece of fiberglass.

The following excerpt from an address to the jury by District Attorney Burton R. Laub in Commonwealth v. Lee, No. 58, September Term, 1944, Erie County (Pennsylvania) Court of Quarter Sessions, a case in which soil evidence was presented, states the argument for the advantage and value of physical evidence.

Now I appreciate the fact that scientific evidence accompanied by descriptions of such technical instruments as spectrographs and microscopes, and co-mingled with the mystery and magic of test-tubes, melting points, boiling points and other confusing names, means little or nothing to the average layman. I confess that they meant little to me until I started looking into the matter for the purposes of this case. Because of this, I should like, with your permission, to reduce the testimony of these scientists to a simple form so that we can all understand what they mean.

Let us take, for example, the testimony concerning paint. Mr. Driscoll told us that he found evidence of five different kinds of paint in the debris which came from the victim's bedclothes and in the debris which came from the defendant's clothing. He told us that these paints existed in the same combination on her bedclothes and his clothing and that, in his opinion, either all of the paint was first on the defendant's clothes and then transferred to the bed or it was on the bed and transferred to his clothes. As another alternative, some of it might have been in both places and then, by contact, became mingled into one mixture of the same elements in both places.

Now we still haven't gotten very far unless we know why he gives us this opinion. You will recall that, on cross-examination, he readily admitted that the types of paint with which we are dealing might exist anywhere and are quite common—although he did say that the black paint in both specimens was of exactly the same chemical composition and that this was a peculiar circumstance since samples of paint from the same bucket are apt to have different chemical compositions. What Mr. Driscoll did say, however, was that though individually these paints might exist anywhere, the probability of their existence in this particular combination was very remote. Now let us see what he means by this. He told us that there was a hard surface red paint, a waxy red paint which he chose to call by another name, there was green paint with an adjacent white layer, blue paint and black paint. For the moment let us forget the word "paint" and talk about something with which we are all familiar.

Suppose that I said to you, "I saw a woman today and she was wearing a red hat," and you answered, "I too saw a woman today and she also was wearing a red hat." Now red hats are extremely common; they may be purchased in any millinery store in the country. Therefore, neither you nor I would jump to the conclusion that we had seen the same woman merely because of the color of her hat. But suppose that I said, "My woman was wearing a bunch of waxy-red cherries on her hat," and you responded, "So was my woman." Now, waxy-red cherries are quite common. A few years back they were an accepted decoration for ladies' hats and it would be fair to assume that every attic in the city would disclose, amid the odds and ends of women's discarded material, at least one bunch of waxy-red cherries. Because of this well-known fact neither you nor I would be willing to venture an opinion that we had seen the same woman. However, we now have developed two points of similarity and are interested in determining whether or not we did see the same person. I describe my woman as having a green cape with a white lining. Garments of this description, while not numerous, may still be found quite commonly; nevertheless, when you reply that your woman was also wearing a green cape with white lining, neither of us have any doubt but that we both saw the same woman. However, we are cautious people and we want more evidence. So you say to me, "My woman was carrying a shiny black pocketbook." Under these circumstances no person of intelligence would conclude that, in a small community such as this, you and I had seen different women. But wait! We have not concluded our comparisons. Suppose that I say, "But my woman was wearing a blue skirt." Now, when you respond that your woman was wearing a blue skirt, both of us will argue to the end of the earth that we have seen the same woman. To clinch matters, however, let us carry our little story a bit farther. Suppose that my woman had dropped her purse on the street and a small chip had fallen off. Because it was so shiny and black, I picked it up. In your case, the woman had bumped her purse against a counter in a near-by department store and you had, for the same reason, picked up a small chip of the black, shiny material which had dropped to the floor. If we take our bits of broken purse to a chemist and he tells us that they are of identical chemical compositions, both you and I will take the witness stand and swear that we saw the same woman. Couple all of these facts with the information that we had seen our woman in the same part of town and at approximately the same time and you will find that we have reduced our probabilities to a certainty.

Now, if we re-translate our colors from clothing back to paint, we have the exact picture as presented here in court. Our red hat is a hard-surface red paint; our cherries are the waxy-red pigment which Mr. Driscoll described. The green cape with the white lining becomes a green paint with an adjacent white layer; the black purse is a shiny black paint and the blue dress becomes, instead, blue paint. That is why Mr. Driscoll had no hesitation in saying that, in his opinion, the two types of debris originated in the same source.

The same type of argument applies with equal force and effect to the expert testimony of Mr. Duggins and Mr. Flach. You will remember how they described the coincidence of brass or bronze particles, cinder and slag material, miscellaneous hair and fibre material, tobacco particles, wood particles, sand grains and salt grains upon the various exhibits. You will recall the colors and textures of the fibres which were found and how they compared. You will remember how, of twenty-four different colors and combinations of fibres, fourteen were present on the defendant's clothes as well as on the bedclothes of the victim.

It would be too obvious and painstaking to translate these combinations of materials in articles of clothing and draw a similar analogy to the one of the woman with the black pocketbook and red cherries. However, anyone can readily see how this evidence has pyramided beyond the point of speculation to the point where we can say with positive conviction that this is the man who made this vicious attack upon Hilda Miller.

We have seen that physical evidence in the form of soil, rocks, minerals, and fossils has limitations as well as advantages. Most important to many problems is what is meant by the word *compare*. It is a word we see many times—soil sample from the shoe of the suspect "compares" with soil samples from the scene of the crime. Alternatively, the rock found at the scene of the crime "compares" with rocks from a quarry in County Galway, Ireland. In examining the meaning that a scientist places on this word, we must remember that no two physical objects can ever, in a theoretical sense, be the same. It is also true that a sample of soil or any other earth material can be said, in an absolute sense, to have come from a single place. All examinations of soil for forensic purposes are aimed at establishing whether there is a very high degree of probability that a sample was or was not derived from a given place. The scientist, based on his training, experience, professional judgment and competency, selects the measurements and observations that will enable him to make such a judgment. By the nature of science, these types of observations and measurements should be reproducible by other professionals undertaking a similar study. There is a constant pressure in the crime laboratory to develop standardized, simple, practical methods for comparison. The problem for forensic geology is to apply methods to soil and related samples that will insure the scientist the opportunity of making a professional judgment with the highest degree of confidence. The methods should not be so detailed that they either become so difficult to perform that they are never used, or, alternatively, are so detailed that comparison is impossible because the scientist is measuring in the range where the theoretical difference between any two objects is reached.

Important in this distinction is the recognition that soils, rocks, minerals, and fossils are very complex mixtures that nature caused to be brought together. In this sense they are far different from manufactured products such as glass, paint, and fibers. Methods that rely on a single measurement of the total sample such as a chemical analysis of the entire sample, or a measure of density distribution of particles in the entire sample, or distribution of sizes of particles in the entire sample, or color of the entire sample may contribute to the professional judgment of comparison, but are seldom sufficient in themselves to provide the basis for a professional judgment of comparison.

This is well illustrated in the case of the bulk chemical analyses. Such analysis may be an excellent method if properly performed, using the most appropriate analytical technique for the comparison of quality-controlled, manufactured products. However, in the case of soils it is not uncommon in analyzing two samples from the same spot to have a few mineral grains from one sample that are missing from the other. If these grains have an unusual concentration of a particular chemical element and the number of these grains in the sample area was small, the analyses should show large differences in the concentration of that element. Alternatively, a chemical analysis for certain elements which are common in minerals may show little difference between a large number of different soils from different places. In practice, the forensic geologist normally searches for the unusual and uncommon particles in soil samples rather than simply measuring a bulk property in attempting to determine whether samples compare.

In the case of the explosion that destroyed part of a plant which manufactured smokeless powder, an unusual rock provided information that was useful during the investigation. In this plant, the powder was extruded from a press and the extruded rods were cut to the desired length. The explosion occurred in the press. After the explosion, an experienced investigator found several small rocks on a screen that was part of the press. They had been in the explosion and must have been mixed into the batch of powder that exploded when squeezed in the press. The presence of these foreign objects in the powder was presumed to have been responsible for the explosion. Rocks with a hardness of greater than approximately 2.5 on the Mohs' hardness scale (Ch. 3) and having a melting temperature greater than 500° C. appear to be able to produce by friction enough heat to detonate some explosives. These rocks met those specifications. The investigators faced the question of whether the rocks were placed in the powder deliberately or by accident. The question was asked, "Where did the rocks come from?" This plant had areas of walks, parking areas, and lawn containing many different kinds of rocks both local and those brought there as cover for paths and aggregate.

The rock fragments removed from the site of the explosion

contained the uncommon feldspar mineral *aventurine,* sometimes called *sunstone.* Although rare, it is quite distinctive and easily recognized. Careful study of the plant area located the place where similar rocks were found. This information was used in the investigation and particularly during the interrogation of suspects about their movements around the plant area prior to the explosion.

The scientist studying earth materials works in a way that is similar to other criminalists. The forensic geologist searches for the unusual rather than the common and bases comparisons on the knowledge that the unusual or combinations that are unusual have a very high degree of probability of being from a single place. In doing this, geologists will use different methods and approaches depending on the kind of soil, the minerals involved, or the size of the individual grains. He will use a number of methods and observations appropriate to the problem and earth material available. Failure to develop sufficient points of similarity or dissimilarity after intensive study usually results from insufficient sample for analysis or failure to observe or measure properties that have evidential value. It is recognized that insufficient sample from the suspect or insufficient or inappropriate sampling commonly results in meaningless expenditure of effort with little likelihood of making a professional contribution.

When the scientist, after performing the study, decides on the basis of his analysis and best professional judgment that certain samples compare or do not compare he must then be prepared to defend that judgment as a scientist in a court of law.

The legal basis for deciding what scientific methods are admissible in a court of law is complex and the forensic geologist should naturally consult an attorney prior to giving testimony. In general three court decisions provide the general rules for admissibility of scientific evidence. In *Frye* (Frye v. United States, 293 Fed. 1013, 1014, D.C. Cir. 1923) the court declared:

Just when a scientific principle or discovery crosses the line between the experimental and demonstrable stages is difficult to define. Somewhere in this twilight zone the evidential force of the principle must be recognized, and while courts will go a long way in admitting expert testimony deduced from a well-recognized scientific principle or discovery, the thing from which the deduction is made must be sufficiently established to have *gained general acceptance in the particular field in which it belongs.* [Italics added]

This case involved the question of admissibility of the Polygraph. As science became more complex and specialized the possibility of finding "general acceptance" in any field by all scientists became a problem. In many scientific fields it is quite uncommon for one specialist to be familiar with the methods used by other specialists. This problem was partly resolved in the *Williams* case (People v. Williams, 164 Cal. App. 2d Supp. 848,331 P. 2d 251, 1958). Here the court in deciding the admissibility of the Nalline test for determining whether a person is under the influence of a narcotic ruled that a showing need only be made that *scientific specialists* in such matters recognized the test and its results to be reliable. There still remained the question of admissibility of scientific evidence where the procedures were devised to meet a particular problem and where there could have been no possibility or opportunity of obtaining prior general acceptance by other specialists. The *Coppolino* case (Coppolino v. State, 223 So. 2d 68, Fla. App. 1968, *app. dismissed* 234 So. 2d 120 Fla. 1969, cert. denied 399 U.S. 927.) involved the admissibility of a previously unknown procedure devised by pathologists to detect a certain chemical in body tissue suspected of causing the death of the victim. The court decided that such tests devised to explore a given problem were admissible provided the expert witness lays a proper foundation for his opinion and explains what accepted principles of analysis he used. Because of the diversity of geologic evidence involving identification of rocks, mineral fossils; use of maps showing rocks, soils, topography; and application of geologic instruments to forensic problems this decision is extremely important.

References

Arthur, O. 1965. *The scientific investigator.* Springfield, Ill.: Charles C. Thomas.

Fox, R. H., and Cunningham, C. L. 1973. *Crime scene search and physical evidence handbook.* Washington, D.C.: U.S. Govt. Prtg. Off., 2700–00221.

Kirk, P. L. 1953. *Crime investigation.* New York: Interscience Publishers.

———. 1974. *Crime investigation.* 2nd ed. (J. I. Thornton, ed.) New York: John Wiley & Sons, Inc.

Neil, M. W., and Warren, F. L., eds. 1962. *Soil teaching symposium, No. 1.* British Academy of Forensic Sciences. London: Sweet and Maxwell, Ltd.

O'Hara, C. E., and Osterburg, J. W. 1972. *Criminalistics.* Bloomington, Ind.: Indiana Univ. Press.

Osterburg, J. W. 1968. *The crime laboratory.* Bloomington, Ind.: Indiana Univ. Press.

Schatz, W., Saale, A., and Halle, D. 1930. Dirt scraped from shoes as a means of identification. *Am. Jour. Police Sci.,* vol. 1, p. 55.

Walls, H. J. 1968. *Forensic science.* New York: Frederick A. Praeger.

———. 1974. *Forensic science.* 2nd ed. New York: Frederick A. Praeger.

3 Origin, Properties, and Distribution of Earth Materials

This chapter and the two that follow on soils and artificial earth materials serve two purposes. The first is to give the background information necessary to understand the various processes and products that provide the material with which the forensic geologist works. The second is to document the diversity of earth materials, that is, the almost infinite kinds of minerals, rocks, fossils, and soils that exist. This documentation is especially important to the purpose of the book because the value of any item of physical evidence in large part depends on the number of kinds available and their distribution. In general, the larger the number the greater will be the statistical probability that a given sample will have properties similar to few, if any, other samples from other locations on this earth.

Rocks and Minerals

Over 2000 individual minerals have been identified. Approximately 200 are discussed in introductory books on mineralogy (Tabs. 3-1 and 3-2). Twenty or so are commonly found in soils but the bulk of the soil will usually contain only some three to five minerals. What is a mineral? Mineralogists

Table 3-1 "LIGHT" MINERALS

	Approximate Chemical Composition	Crystal System	Specific Gravity	Mohs' Hardness	Common Use
Beryl	$Be_3Al_2(Si_6O_{18})$	Hexagonal	2.75–2.8	7½–8	Source of Be, gemstone
Calcite	$CaCO_3$	Rhombohedral	2.71	3	Cement, quicklime
Dolomite	$CaMg(CO_3)_2$	Rhombohedral	2.85	3½–4	Soil conditioner
Feldspar (Plagioclase)					
Albite [Ab]	$Na(AlSi_3O_8)-Ab_{90}-An_{10}$	Triclinic	2.62	6	Ceramics, cleaning powder
Oligoclase	$Ab_{90}-An_{10}-Ab_{70}-An_{30}$	Triclinic	2.65	6	
Andesine	$Ab_{70}-An_{30}-Ab_{50}-An_{50}$	Triclinic	2.69	6	
Labradorite	$Ab_{50}-An_{50}-Ab_{30}-An_{70}$	Triclinic	2.71	6	
Bytownite	$Ab_{30}-An_{70}-Ab_{10}-An_{90}$	Triclinic	2.74	6	
Anorthite [An]	$Ab_{10}An_{90}-CaAl_2Si_2O_8$	Triclinic	2.76	6	
Feldspar (Potassium)					
Orthoclase	$K(AlSi_3O_8)$	Monoclinic	2.57	6	Porcelain, cleaning powder
Microcline	$K(AlSi_3O_8)$	Triclinic	2.54–2.57	6	
Glauconite	$K_2(Mg,Fe)_2Al_6(Si_4O_{10})_3(OH)_{12}$	Monoclinic	2.3±	2	Water softener
Gypsum	$CaSO_4 \cdot 2H_2O$	Monoclinic	2.32	2	Plaster of paris
Halite	$NaCl$	Isometric	2.16	2½	Rocksalt, deiceing salt, table salt
Quartz	SiO_2	Rhombohedral	2.65	7	Glass, radio crystal
Talc	$Mg_3(Si_4O_{10})(OH)_2$	Monoclinic	2.7–2.8	1	Optical equipment, soapstone, talcum powder, filler

Table 3-2 "HEAVY MINERALS"

	Approximate Chemical Composition	Crystal System	Specific Gravity	Mohs' Hardness	Common Use
Actinolite	$Ca_2(Mg,Fe)_5(Si_8O_{22})(OH)_2$	Monoclinic	3.0–3.2	5–6	
Anatase	TiO_2	Tetragonal	3.9	$5\frac{1}{2}$–6	Source of Ti
Andalusite	Al_2SiO_5	Orthorhombic	3.16–3.20	$7\frac{1}{2}$	Refractory
Anhydrite	$CaSO_4$	Orthorhombic	2.89–2.98	3–$3\frac{1}{2}$	Soil conditioner
Apatite	$Ca_5(F,Cl,OH)(PO_4)_3$	Hexagonal	3.15–3.20	5	Gemstone, fertilizer
Aragonite	$CaCO_3$	Orthorhombic	2.95	$3\frac{1}{2}$–4	
Augite	$(Ca,Na)(Mg,Fe,Al)(Si,Al)_2O_6$	Monoclinic	3.2–3.4	1.67–1.73	
Biotite	$K(Mg,Fe)_3(AlSi_3O_{10})(OH)_2$	Monoclinic	2.8–3.2	$2\frac{1}{2}$–3	
Corundum	Al_2O_3	Rhombohedral	4.02	9	Gemstone, abrasive
Diopside	$CaMg(Si_2O_6)$	Monoclinic	3.2–3.3	5–6	
Enstatite	$Mg_2(Si_2O_6)$	Orthorhombic	3.2–3.5	$5\frac{1}{2}$	
Epidote	$Ca_2(Al,Fe)Al_2O(SiO_4) \cdot (Si_2O_7)(OH)$	Monoclinic	3.35–3.45	6–7	
Fluorite	CaF_2	Isometric	3.18	4	Flux for steel, glass
Garnet	A complex silicate	Isometric	3.5–4.3	$6\frac{1}{2}$–$7\frac{1}{2}$	Gemstone, abrasive
Hematite	Fe_2O_3	Rhombohedral	5.26	$5\frac{1}{2}$–$6\frac{1}{2}$	Pigments, polishes
Hornblende	$Ca_2Na(Mg,Fe^2)_4(Al,Fe^3,Ti)_3 \cdot Si_8O_{22}(O,OH)_2$	Monoclinic	3.2	5–6	
Hypersthene	$(Mg,Fe)_2(Si_2O_6)$	Orthorhombic	3.4–3.5	5–6	
Ilmenite	$FeTiO_3$	Rhombohedral	4.7	$5\frac{1}{2}$–6	Source of Ti for paint and pigment
Kyanite	Al_2SiO_5	Triclinic	3.56–3.66	5–7	Refractory
Magnetite	Fe_3O_4	Isometric	5.18	6	Iron ore
Malachite	$Cu_2CO_3(OH)_2$	Monoclinic	3.9–4.03	$3\frac{1}{2}$–4	
Marcasite	FeS_2	Orthorhombic	4.89	6–$6\frac{1}{2}$	
Muscovite	$KAl_2(AlSi_3O_{10})(OH)_2$	Monoclinic	2.75–3.1	2–$2\frac{1}{2}$	Insulation and filler

Table 3-2 "HEAVY MINERALS" (continued)

	Approximate Chemical Composition	Crystal System	Specific Gravity	Mohs' Hardness	Common Use
Olivine	$(Mg,Fe)_2SiO_4$	Orthorhombic	3.27–4.37	6½–7	Gemstone
Pyrite	FeS_2	Isometric	5.02	6–6½	Fool's gold
Rutile	TiO_2	Tetragonal	4.18–4.25	6–6½	Welding rod coating, source of Ti for paint pigment
Sphene	$CaTiO(SiO_4)$	Monoclinic	3.40–3.55	5–5½	
Spinel	$MgAl_2O_4$	Isometric	3.6–4.0	8	
Staurolite	$Fe_2Al_9O_6(SiO_4)_4(O,OH)_2$	Orthorhombic	3.65–3.75	7–7½	Gemstone ornament
Tourmaline	$(Na,K)(Fe,Mg,Li,Al)_3Al_6(BO_3)_3(Si_6O_{18})(OH)_4$	Rhombohedral	3.0–3.25	7–7½	Gemstone
Tremolite	$Ca_2Mg_5(Si_8O_{22})(OH)_2$	Monoclinic	3.0–3.3	5–6	
Zircon	$ZrSiO_4$	Tetragonal	4.68	7½	Gemstone, source of Zr
Zoisite	$CaAl(SiO)(OH)$	Orthorhombic	3.35	6	
Topaz	$Al_2(SiO_4)(F,OH)_2$	Orthorhombic	3.4–3.6	8	Gemstone

agree that a mineral is a naturally occurring substance with a characteristic internal structure determined by a regular arrangement of atoms or ions within it, and with a chemical composition and physical properties that are either fixed or that vary within a definite range. There is a difficulty in applying this definition to some of the particles we see in soils. For example, coal is naturally occurring but does not have a fixed chemical composition. Volcanic glass is naturally occurring but lacks an orderly internal structure. Many man-made grains such as silicon carbide abrasive are not naturally occurring, but do have the other mineral-like characteristics.

The geologist trained in the identification of minerals normally can recognize at sight twenty to fifty of the most common minerals and some of the less common ones that have very distinctive properties. In doing this the identification is made in much the same way that a forester identifies trees or a zoologist identifies animals. A characteristic or series of characteristics is observed and compared in the mind with similar material seen in the past. The characteristics of minerals that are commonly observed, usually with the aid of a lens or low power *binocular* microscope (Fig. 3-1), are color, luster, the way the mineral breaks—called cleavage or fracture—and streak, that is the color of the mineral when it is finely divided. Some minerals are magnetic and can be lifted with a magnet. Minerals have different densities and this property can be used for identification. The boundary between the so called "heavy" and "light" minerals is generally drawn at 2.89 grams per cubic centimeter. In addition, the form of crystal faces results from the orderly internal structure of atoms and ions (Fig. 3-2). Many minerals crystallize with the same arrangement of crystal faces. However, the crystal form is useful, when combined with other properties, in recognizing some of the mineral species (Fig. 3-3).

In most forensic work the size of the individual mineral grains is small and the most significant information is often obtained from the unusual and uncommon minerals. Thus, other methods are commonly used. When minerals cannot be identified positively with the low-power binocular microscope the geologist uses a polarizing or *petrographic microscope* (Fig. 3-1).

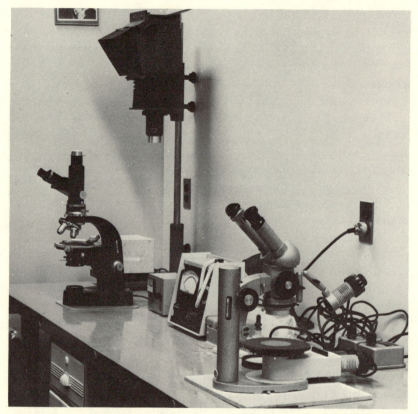

Figure 3-1   Laboratory showing binocular and petrographic microscopes.

This microscope differs from an ordinary biological microscope in that it has filters capable of polarizing the light, a rotating stage, and attachments for viewing the characteristic effects on light that has passed through minerals.

A common technique in the study of rocks or similar material is to prepare a *thin section* for study under the petrographic microscope. Thin sections are prepared by grinding the rock that has been cemented to a glass microscope slide so thin that it is actually transparent. This permits the scientist to see and identify the minerals and how they fit together.

If minerals in the sand and silt fractions are identified there is generally a predominance of quartz and feldspar with some minor components. The clay fraction—that generally smaller than 2 microns—will, however, be commonly composed of a different group of minerals known as the clay minerals (Tab. 3-3). The general trend in change of mineral composition with particle size is shown in Figure 3-4.

Minerals, especially the small-sized ones, are commonly identified using x-ray techniques (Fig. 3-5) or by differential thermal analysis.

Many other instruments that are useful in identifying and studying the various minerals are available to the geologist. Of particular value is the electron microscope and scanning elec-

Figure 3-2   Quartz crystals showing the characteristic crystal faces. *Courtesy of Richard Tripp*

Isometric	Three axes, all the same length, and all intersecting at right angles.	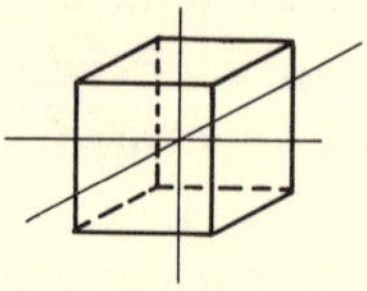
Tetragonal	Three axes, two of equal length and one unequal, all intersecting at right angles.	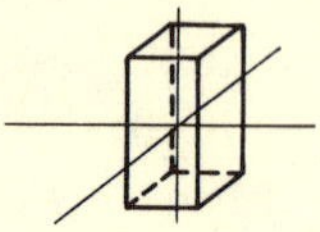
Hexagonal	Four axes, three of equal length, in the same plane, meeting at angles of 120°, the fourth not equal in length and intersecting the plane of the others at 90°.	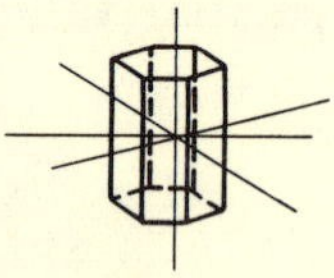
Orthorhombic	Three axes, all unequal in length, and all meeting in right angles.	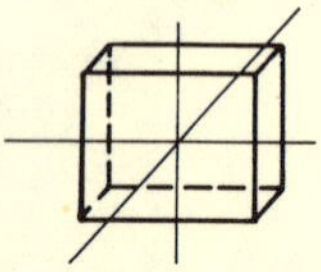
Monoclinic	Three axes, all unequal in length, two of which intersect in a right angle.	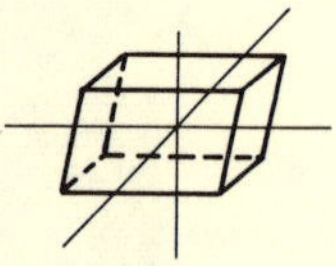
Triclinic	Three axes, all unequal in length, with none meeting in right angles.	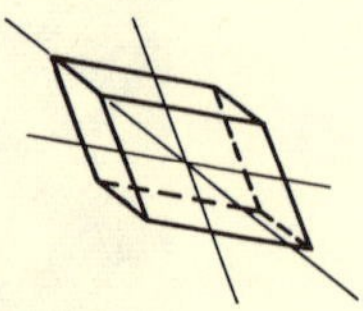

Figure 3-3 Crystal systems.

tron microscope (SEM). With these instruments it is possible to examine particles enlarged over 100,000 times, thus permitting identification of small mineral particles sometimes adhering to the surface of a larger mineral grain.

Although there are thousands of kinds of minerals it is well to remember that there are very large numbers of variation within each kind. This can be easily appreciated by examining one of the many books that list and discuss the properties of minerals.

Rocks are aggregates of minerals. They may be natural as in the case of granite, or artificial, such as concrete. There are three main ways in which rocks are formed: by *igneous, metamorphic, and sedimentary,* processes. The process and the material from which the rock is made determine the minerals that will be present and the texture, that is, the size, shape, and the way in which the minerals fit together in the rock.

Igneous rocks are formed by the melting of older rocks or parts of older rocks deep within the earth at temperatures commonly in excess of 600° C. When the melt cools, minerals grow within the liquid and ultimately a solid mass of minerals forms.

Table 3-3 SOME OF THE MORE COMMON CLAY MINERALS

Silicate Clays	Mineral	Comments
1:1 *	Kaolinite	A mineral consisting of alternating layers of silica tetrahedra and alumina octahedra.
1:1	Halloysite	A hydrated form of kaolinite.
1:1	Allophane	Mineral with random arrangements of silica tetrahedra and metallic octahedra.
2:1	Illite (Muscovite)	A general name for mica-like clays.
2:1	Glauconite	Illite-like mineral with much replacement of Al by Fe and Mg.
2:1	Vermiculite	Alteration product of mica. Related to micas. Considerable variation in chemical composition.
2:1	Montmorillonite	A finely divided mica-like clay which expands when moist.
2:1	Chlorite	Mica-like material interstratified with brucite.
Hydroxide Clays		
—	Gibbsite	A form of aluminum hydroxide.

* 1:1 One layer of silica tetrahedra and one layer of alumina octahedra (known as 1:1 silicates).
  2:1 One layer of alumina octahedra sandwiched between 2 layers of silica tetrahedra (known as 2:1 silicates).

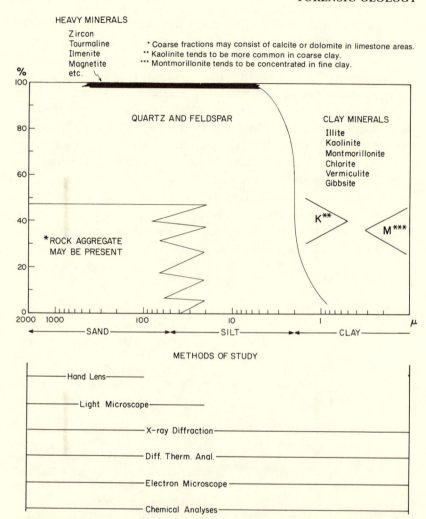

HEAVY MINERALS

Zircon
Tourmaline   * Coarse fractions may consist of calcite or dolomite in limestone areas.
Ilmenite   ** Kaolinite tends to be more common in coarse clay.
Magnetite   *** Montmorillonite tends to be concentrated in fine clay.
etc.

QUARTZ AND FELDSPAR

CLAY MINERALS

Illite
Kaolinite
Montmorillonite
Chlorite
Vermiculite
Gibbsite

K**

M***

*ROCK AGGREGATE
MAY BE PRESENT

2000   1000   100   10   1   μ

◄—————— SAND ——————► ◄————— SILT —————► ◄— CLAY ——►

METHODS OF STUDY

——— Hand Lens ———
——— Light Microscope ———
——— X-ray Diffraction ———
——— Diff. Therm. Anal. ———
——— Electron Microscope ———
——— Chemical Analyses ———

Figure 3-4   Sizes of soil minerals. Coarse fractions generally consist of quartz, feldspar, perhaps a little mica, rock aggregates, and some heavy minerals. Progressing from left to right, minerals present in the sands give way to a set of minerals having different properties and characteristics—generally consisting of illite (mica), kaolinite, chlorite, and others. Minerals in the coarse fractions can be identified by a number of techniques, but the clay minerals, because of their small size, require special procedures as listed. This diagram can be used as a general guide, but it would not necessarily be applicable for special situations such as limestone deposits or soils of the humid tropics. The main clay minerals present in soils and sediments are listed in Table 7-1.

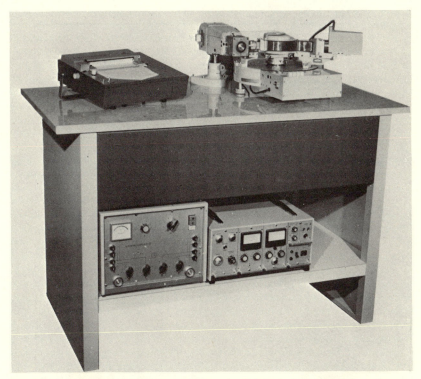

Figure 3-5   Instrument for identifying minerals by X-ray diffraction. *Courtesy of John E. Enderlein, ES Industries*

When the liquid flows out on the surface of the earth as it often does from a volcano, it is called *lava*. When the melted rock is still within the earth it is called *magma*. Some igneous rocks form within the earth by the slow cooling of magma. Most impressive is the almost unlimited number of variations in the kinds of igneous rocks (Fig. 3-6). What this means is that igneous rocks are found with wide variations in the kinds and amounts of different minerals and the variations in textures. This is not difficult to understand when we remember that the magma was formed by the melting of different types of older rocks or in many cases selectively melting only parts of older rocks. Thus, magmas and lavas begin with a wide variety of chemical compositions. As these liquids cool, minerals begin to crystallize. The

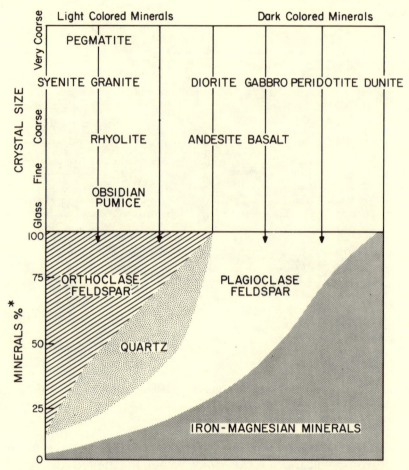

Figure 3-6   Names and general composition of some igneous rocks.

minerals that will form depend on the original chemical composition and how fast the liquid cools. During the cooling, different minerals form at different temperatures and some of the already formed minerals change to new minerals as the temperature drops. Because the minerals that grow at any given temperature have a different chemical composition than that of the liquid, the chemical composition of the liquid changes with cooling. For example, if a mineral that needs 10 percent iron is formed and the liquid has only 5 percent iron, the liquid will generally have less than 5 percent iron after the mineral has formed. After some of the minerals that form at the higher temperatures have already grown, a mush of liquid and crystals will exist. That liquid will have a different chemical composition from the original liquid. If, as commonly happens, the remaining liquid is drawn off or separated from the early formed crystals, the separated liquid will act like a new magma and will form the minerals that would be expected from a magma of the new composition. It is for these reasons, original melting or selective melting of a wide variety of original minerals and the different minerals that can be formed during cooling, that we have on the earth igneous rocks of an almost unlimited number of possible mineral compositions.

The textures of igneous rocks, that is, the size and arrangement of minerals within the rock, depend on the original chemical composition of the magma and how rapidly or slowly the magma cools. A lava that flows out on the earth's surface and thus cools relatively fast will generally have small-size crystals, while a magma that cools within the earth, surrounded by rocks that will be hot and act as insulators, will cool slowly. The slow-cooling magma generally will develop larger crystals. In some rocks the early-formed minerals may grow to larger size, while the later minerals that form at lower temperatures are smaller. Such a rock is called a *porphyry* and has larger crystals set in a mass of finer crystals. It is not uncommon for such rocks to form when magma cools slowly within the earth until the early minerals have first had a chance to grow. At this time the minerals and the remaining liquid flow to the surface of the earth and appear as quickly cooling lava. Igneous rocks with the same mineral composition can appear with a very large number of textures. One standard textbook on *Igneous Rock Petrography*, that is, the description of igneous rocks, lists over 750 different rock types and each of these has a range of mineral composition and textures within each type. Anyone who has looked along a stream paved with boulders and cobbles in an area of igneous rocks or a wall made of igneous rocks (Fig. 3-7) quickly realizes that each of the rocks is different from the others and that the differences can easily be recognized. Such an observa-

Figure 3-7 Wall made of some of the different kinds of granite, an igneous rock.

tion helps us to appreciate the almost unlimited diversity of igneous rocks.

Sedimentary rocks, like most rocks, are made up of minerals. In the case of these rocks, the minerals come from the destruction and breakup of older rocks. This destruction takes place by weathering and the broken particles or dissolved elements from the older rock may be carried away by water, wind, ice, or some other means, and deposited at another location on or near the surface. This deposit or sediment is then bound together into a solid rock when new minerals grow within the voids between the once loose particles and cement the particles together. In this way a sedimentary rock is formed. Sediments may form in two ways and are generally described as two different kinds, *chemical* and *detrital*. The chemical sediments are deposited from waters that carry dissolved chemical elements (Tab. 3-4). Sea water provides a familiar example. If sea water is concentrated by evaporation, a variety of minerals will grow and settle to the bottom of the ocean. The most common mineral that forms from sea water is halite; that is, common salt. Swim in the ocean on a dry day and let the sea water evaporate as you dry in the sun. Watch the crystals of the mineral halite (sodium chloride) grow on your skin. Look closely and you will see that several other minerals have also formed. Animals and plants commonly will use elements in water to form minerals such as the shell of a clam or the tooth of a fish. Even some of the simple algae grow minerals within their bodies which fall to the sea bottom when the algae die. The number of different minerals that have formed from sea, lake, river or spring water or have been formed within the tissue of plants and animals is very large. These minerals make up the particles of most of the chemical sediments and chemical sedimentary rocks.

The appearance of a rock in an area where it could not have originated often leads to substantial evidence. A herd of prize cattle was stolen from a farm in Missouri and was suspected of having been transported to a ranch in Montana. The brands had been altered. However, the owner was positive that he recognized his cattle on the suspect's Montana ranch. An examination of the bed of the cattle truck owned by the suspect revealed abundant fragments of chert, a chemical sedimentary rock, mixed with the manure. This chert was identifiable as originat-

Table 3-4 SEDIMENTARY ROCKS—CHEMICAL ROCK TYPES

Rock Name	Composition of Major Minerals	Common Origin
Limestone	Calcite $CaCO_3$	Shells of marine organisms
Dolomite	Dolomite $CaMg(CO_3)_2$	Alteration of limestone
Chert	Quartz SiO_2	Opal shells of marine organisms and chemical precipitation
Gypsum	Gypsum $CaSO_4 2H_2O$	Evaporation of sea water
Rock salt	Halite $NaCl$	
Coal	Altered plant material	Accumulated plant material

ing in Missouri. The suspect denied that his truck had ever been outside the state of Montana. Further study demonstrated that the chert found on the bed of the truck compared with that found at the foot of the cattle loading ramp on the Missouri farm. Many pieces of chert had apparently been picked up on the hoofs of the cattle and carried onto the truck during the larceny and remained there until discovered by the investigators.

Detrital sediments form from the broken parts of older rocks (Tab. 3-5). During weathering and the breakup of older rocks, many new minerals grow from some of the original minerals. These new minerals plus the broken minerals from the older rock are carried away by wind, rivers, waves, and shore currents, gravity and glacial ice, and dropped, to form masses of sediment. The forms that these masses of sediment may take are many and varied. For example, a river may drop sediment on the stream bed or along and over its banks during flood. When the river reaches a lake or sea, it will drop much of the sediment being carried in the form of a delta. The delta of the Mississippi River on which the city of New Orleans is built was made from sediment dropped by the river over thousands of years. Waves and shore currents may carry sediment to form beaches and some of the sediment may be carried off shore to fall on the floor of the sea. Wind blowing on to a shoreline may pick up sand from a beach and drop it as dunes on the land side of the beach.

Table 3-5 SEDIMENTARY ROCKS—DETRITAL ROCK TYPES

Rock Name	Major Minerals	Texture
Conglomerate	Rounded fragments of rock	Coarse grained, over 2 mm.
Breccia	Angular fragments of rock	
Sandstone	Quartz	Medium grained, $\frac{1}{16}$–2 mm.
Arkose	Quartz, more than 25% feldspar	
Siltstone or shale	Quartz and clay minerals	Fine grained, $\frac{1}{256}$–$\frac{1}{16}$ mm.
Mudstone or shale	Quartz and clay minerals	Very fine grained, less than $\frac{1}{256}$ mm.

The same process takes place anywhere grains of sand or silt are not protected by plants and can be easily picked up by the wind, such as on a desert. A landslide caused by gravity may move down a hill and form a mass of sediment on the valley below. This same process takes place slowly on most hillslopes and sediment creeps down the hill under its own weight, thus cleaning off the hills and moving sediment to a mass at the base of the hill. Glacial ice, when it melts, drops all the particles of rocks and minerals it carried, forming a ridge of sediment called a *moraine*. If the melting is rapid, the rock and mineral debris will be dropped, littering the landscape with a blanket of sediment.

Some years ago a gas works in northern Massachusetts experienced what appeared to be repeated acts of vandalism. The coal they used, which was mined in Pennsylvania and transported to Massachusetts by both rail and water, contained boulders and cobbles of igneous rocks that were destroying the grates in the furnace. The rocks could have been introduced into the coal from a number of places between the mine and the plant. Examination of the rocks showed that they were derived from an area north of the place where the coal was stored near the plant and had markings indicative of having been moved by glacial ice. The glacially deposited soil on which the coal was stored had similar boulders and cobbles. Upon investigation at the coal storage area it was found that the coal shovel operator commonly drank alcoholic beverages on the job. At these times he tended to misjudge the depth to the bottom of the coal and scooped up some of the underlying glacial deposits. The situation was quickly remedied.

The sediment dropped by glacial ice or gravity tends to contain grains in all the available sizes (Tab. 3-6). In the case of glacial deposits this may be a sediment composed of everything from boulders the size of a house to the finest clay, all mixed together. Such a sediment is said to be poorly sorted, that is, it is composed of particles of many different sizes. When sediment is moved by a fluid such as water, as in the case of a river, lake, sea shore, or by the wind, the size of particles that can be carried depends on the velocity and viscosity of the fluid, the size, shape, and density of the particle. Water is more viscous

Table 3-6 VARIOUS SIZE GRADE SCALES IN COMMON USE

Udden-Wentworth	φ values	German Scale † (after Atterberg)	USDA and Soil Sci. Soc. Amer.	U.S. Corps Eng., Dept. Army and Bur. Reclamation ‡
		(Blockwerk)		
Cobbles		—200 mm—	Cobbles	Boulders
			—80 mm—	
——64 mm——	−6			——10 in.——
		Gravel		Cobbles
Pebbles		(Kies)		——3 in.——
——4 mm——	−2		Gravel	Gravel
				——4 mesh——
Granules				Coarse sand
——2 mm——	−1	—2 mm—	——2 mm——	——10 mesh——
Very coarse sand			Very coarse sand	
——1 mm——	0		——1 mm——	
Coarse sand			Coarse sand	Medium sand
		Sand		
——0.5 mm——	1		——0.5 mm——	——40 mesh——
Medium sand			Medium sand	
——0.25 mm——	2		——0.25 mm——	
Fine sand			Fine sand	Fine sand
——0.125 mm——	3		——0.10 mm——	
Very fine sand				
			Very fine sand	——200 mesh——
——0.0625 mm——	4	—0.0625 mm—		
			——0.05 mm——	
Silt		Silt		
			Silt	Fines
——0.0039 mm——	8			
		—0.002 mm—	——0.002 mm——	
Clay		Clay (Ton)	Clay	

† Subdivisions of sand sizes omitted.

‡ Mesh numbers are for U.S. Standard Sieves: 4 mesh = 4.76 mm, 10 mesh = 2.00 mm, 40 mesh = 0.42 mm, 200 mesh = 0.074 mm.

than air and can move a particle easier than can air. In general, the faster the current is moving, the larger the particle that can be moved in any given fluid. If the current slows, then the particles that are too large to be carried will settle out and be deposited. When a river enters a lake, it ceases to flow as a river and all the particles settle to the bottom. Naturally, the larger particles will settle out first and the finest will settle more slowly. But not all minerals or rocks have the same density. A dense mineral will settle faster than a lighter mineral of the same size and shape. Thus deposits of sediment that were carried by fluids generally tend to be sorted, that is, they will be composed of a limited number of sizes. In the same way, minerals of different density may be concentrated. It is in this way that the so-called placer gold deposits are formed. Gold has a very high density, ranging from over fifteen to almost twenty times the density of water. Compared with the common lighter minerals, it is easily dropped when the velocity of the current falls. The gold, because of its density, should settle out of water at the same time as a grain of relatively light quartz many times its size. If the larger grains of quartz and the other common light minerals are not present, the gold will be deposited and concentrated along with the other very heavy minerals. These placer concentrations are the places where gold and other heavy minerals can be easily mined in river deposits.

Sorting and separations by size, shape, and density of minerals is a natural process and results in sediments that differ widely over short distances in mineral composition. When we remember that each river is flowing over rocks that differ widely in mineral composition and texture and that at any place on a river the minerals or combinations of minerals that are possible are all those that might be found upstream, it is no wonder that the possible variations in mineral composition, mineral or rock particle size, and texture are almost unlimited and will change rapidly from place to place.

Sediments deposited by rivers, wind, waves, and short currents, gravity, and glacial ice, that is, detrital sediments, may be turned into solid rock. This takes place when water moving through the holes or spaces between the grains deposits new minerals which precipitate out of the water within these spaces. The new minerals are called *mineral cement.* Thus a sedimentary rock has three parts, the particles of minerals and rocks, the air or water filled spaces between the particles called *pores* and the cement minerals that grow within the pores and bind the particles together. The chemical composition of the mineral cement and texture and amount of these minerals add the possibility of additional variability to sedimentary rocks.

The formation of rocks by nature is a continuing process and has been going on since the beginning of the earth, nearly four and one-half billion years ago. Thus many of the rocks and minerals that become part of the new sedimentary rock may have been part of older sedimentary rocks and were not derived directly from igneous rocks. These are sometimes called second or many-cycled particles. With this in mind it is important to recognize that minerals differ in their resistance to wear and also differ in the ease with which they dissolve. For example, a relatively soft mineral such as gypsum, which has a hardness of only 2 on the Mohs' scale (Fig. 3-8), will be abraded and ground to smaller particles much faster than a relatively hard mineral such as quartz during the same amount of transport by a stream or wind. Thus we would expect the softer minerals to be more common in the finer sizes or be eliminated during transport. More important, minerals differ in their resistance to dissolving. The resistance of a given mineral depends not only on the mineral but also on the chemical composition of the ground or river water. Slightly acid ground waters will dissolve the mineral calcite much faster than most other minerals but will have little effect on quartz. Thus the minerals that are preserved depend not only on the minerals present, but also on the climate, or more precisely, all the different climates and waters that the minerals have been exposed to during their history. In addition, minerals are often subjected to the effects of animals. An earthworm ingests masses of mineral particles. While they are within the digestive tract of the worm, minerals are subjected to many physical and chemical changes that cause the destruction of some while others come through relatively unchanged. Thus, sediments that have been subjected to many cycles of weathering and transport will have those minerals that are resistant to decay and dissolving whereas those that are less resistant will be scarce. Most sedimentary rocks will have minerals and rocks that represent mixtures of some fresh material and some material that

INDEX MINERALS   **Common Objects**

Figure 3-8   The Mohs' scale of hardness.

has been around long enough so that only the most resistant minerals are preserved.

Igneous and sedimentary rocks may become buried by younger material and thus be carried down deep within the earth. This is possible because some areas of the earth are actually sinking. Today, southern Louisiana is sinking at such a rapid rate that sediments deposited only a few million years ago are now covered by thousands of feet of sediments. At the same time, other areas of the earth are rising. Rock on top of mountains along the west coast of California were deep beneath sea level and covered by sediments a few million years ago. When igneous or sedimentary rocks are buried deep within the crust of the earth, they are subjected to very high temperatures and pressures. The temperature within the outer part of the earth increases approximately one degree Centigrade for each 100 meters below the surface, and the pressure is at least equal to the weight of the overlying rocks. When sedimentary or igneous rocks are subjected to these higher pressures and temperatures, new minerals grow within the rocks and the rocks become changed. Such rocks are then called *metamorphic* (Tab. 3-7).

As would be expected, the new minerals that grow to form metamorphic rock are those that require high temperatures and pressures and generally are not formed at or near the surface of the earth. In addition to the new minerals, the textures that are produced differ from those found in the original rocks and are highly distinctive. A shale originally composed of fine detrital particles may become a mass of mica crystals where the micas are arranged parallel to each other and the rock is then called a mica schist. In addition, new minerals such as garnet may form within the schist. The minerals that form will depend on the original sediment and the pressure and temperature conditions to which the rock has been subjected. Again we see a process which causes diversity in the kinds of rocks.

The result of all these processes is to produce an almost unlimited number of possibilities in the kinds of rocks (Fig. 3-9).

Table 3-7   METAMORPHIC ROCKS

Rock Name	Texture	Major Minerals	Derived From
Slate	Fine-grained; smooth, slaty cleavage; grains not visible	Clay minerals, chlorite, and minor micas	Shale
Schist	Medium-grained; grains visible; platey minerals parallel to each other.	Various platy minerals, such as micas, graphite, and talc, plus quartz and plagioclase feldspar	Shale, basalt
Gneiss	Medium- to coarse-grained; alternating bands of light and dark minerals	Quartz, feldspars, garnet, micas, amphiboles, occasionally pyroxenes	Shale, granite
Quartzite	Medium-grained	Quartz	Sandstone
Marble	Medium- to coarse-grained	Quartz, calcite, dolomite	Limestone or dolostone

Figure 3-9   Wall made of kinds of gneiss, a metamorphic rock.

When we look at rocks exposed on the surface of the earth we are immediately impressed with this diversity. It may be argued that no two samples are alike in a theoretical sense. This is certainly true. However, in a practical sense, the number of different kinds of rocks where the differences can be recognized by simple observation or simple tests made by a trained observer is almost unlimited.

Fossils

Rocks, particularly the sedimentary rocks, often contain the preserved parts of once living animals and plants. Such objects are called *fossils* and they can be used for a variety of purposes (Fig. 3-10). The geologist uses fossils to determine the age of the rock. This is possible because plants and animals have changed

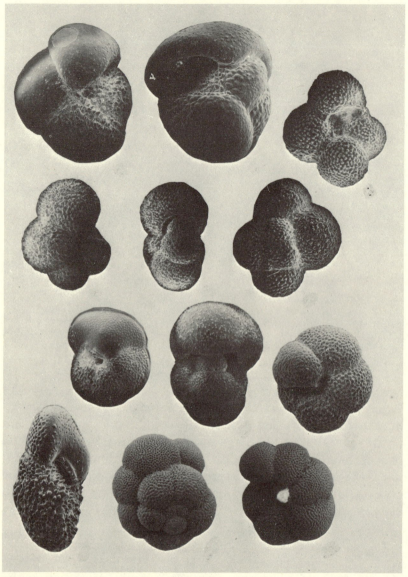

Figure 3-10   Some of the variations found in foraminifera, one of the kinds of microscopic fossils. *Courtesy of R. K. Olsson*

drastically through time because of evolution. Thus, we find certain fossils preserved in rocks of one geologic age and absent in rocks of earlier or later ages. Some fossils are found in rocks that were deposited over a longer period of time because the evolution of those plants or animals took place slowly. In other cases a particular fossil or group of fossils survived only a short span of time and will be found in rocks that were formed during that short time span.

The oldest fossils have been found in rocks as old as three and one half billion years (Fig. 3-11). However, most of these early life forms did not produce hard parts such as shells and few are preserved. Approximately 550 to 650 million years ago animals had evolved to the point where many were producing hard parts. In sedimentary rocks formed from that time to the present these parts are commonly preserved.

Just as living animals and plants today are found and concentrated in certain places, this has also been true in the past. For example, particular oysters may live in waters that have a certain temperature or narrow range of temperatures. They will live only in sea water that is not too diluted with fresh water or too concentrated and they require a sea bottom that has hard places for them to attach and grow. Ancient animals and plants also restricted themselves to particular environments. Thus two fossils that were living at the same time may be found in different environments. For these reasons we find great diversity of fossils in rocks. Over 1,090,000 different species of fossils from animals that leave hard parts have been recognized. This does not include the plants. Some are relatively common and some are very scarce. They are identified by *paleontologists,* that is, persons trained in the study of fossils, in much the same way a biologist identifies living animals. The biologist compares the living animal with known animals and sometimes makes measurements on the animal that permit separating one animal from another. It is a highly specialized business and most paleontologists will become competent at recognizing at sight only one group of fossils such as dinosaur bones or corals or the small microscopic creatures such as diatoms. Most well-trained paleontologists can

Systems	Series	Millions of Yrs. Ago	Evolutionary Events
CENOZOIC			
Quaternary	Pleistocene		Man appears
		— 3 —	
	Pliocene		Many elephants, horses, large carnivores Mammals diversify
	Miocene		
Tertiary		—22—	Grasses become abundant Grazing animals spread
	Oligocene		
	Eocene		First horses appear
	Paleocene		Mammals develop, expand
		—62—	Dinosaurs die off
MESOZOIC			
Cretaceous			Flowering plants appear
		—130—	
Jurassic			Many dinosaurs
		—180—	Birds appear
Triassic			Primitive mammals appear Many conifers and cycads
		—230—	Dinosaurs appear
PALEOZOIC			
Permian			Reptiles spread; conifers develop
		—280—	
Pennsylvanian			First primitive reptiles; abundant insects
			Many coal-forming forests
Mississippian			Fishes diversify
		—340—	Amphibians appear
Devonian			Forests appear
		—400—	
Silurian			First land plants and animals
		—450—	
Ordovician			First fish appear
		— 500 —	
Cambrian			Abundant marine invertebrates
		—570—	
PRECAMBRIAN		4500	Simple marine plants evolve Beginnings of the earth

Figure 3-11 The geologic time table.

identify many of the fossils when they have examples for comparison that have been collected and identified.

We will see that fossils have many specific applications in forensic work. However, it is well to remember that they add another kind of diversity to rocks that facilitates the comparison of samples or may be used to determine the locality from which a sample was picked up. This is especially true for the very small fossils which can only be seen with the aid of a microscope.

Coal

Coal is a rock composed for the most part of the fossil remains of plants. Similar material is forming today in swamps. Detrital mineral grains are usually carried into swamps and these become mixed with the plant material to add impurities in the coal. As the swamp sediment becomes buried, it changes from the original sedimentary rock to a metamorphic rock with the stages or rank called: Plant material → Peat → Lignite → Bituminous Coal → Anthracite Coal. This is called the coal series (Tab. 3-8). The organic material itself is formed mainly of carbon, hydrogen, and oxygen, with small amounts of nitrogen, sulfur, and other trace elements. As the coal rises in rank, that is, becomes metamorphosed, the carbon content increases and the oxygen and hydrogen decrease, creating an almost unlimited number of coal kinds.

Coal fragments are sometimes found in the sweepings from automobile floorboards, in the soils of our older cities and many

Table 3-8 APPROXIMATE CHEMICAL COMPOSITION OF COAL, LIGNITE, PEAT AND WOOD
(Clarke, 1924)

	Carbon	Hydrogen %	Oxygen
Wood	50	6	43
Peat	55	6	36
Lignite	73	5	21
Bituminous Coal	84	6	9
Anthracite Coal	94	3	3

other locations removed from the original mines or outcrops because of the common use of the material as fuel. The presence of coal, the amount of coal in the sample, the kind of coal as determined by microscopic studies of the contained fossils, minerals, and textures have proved to be useful to the forensic geologist. In addition, coals have received considerable study as fossil fuels and it is possible to differentiate the almost unlimited kinds of coal sometimes using differential thermal analyses and detailed chemical composition in addition to the microscopic work.

References

Blatt, H., Middleton, G., and Murray, R. C. 1972. *Origin of sedimentary rocks.* Englewood Cliffs, N.J.: Prentice-Hall, Inc.

Clarke, F. W. 1924. *Data of geochemistry.* 5th ed. U.S. Geological Survey Bull. 770.

Flint, R. F. 1971. *Glacial and quaternary geology.* New York: John Wiley and Sons.

Gilluly, J., Waters, A. C., and Woodford, A. O. 1968. *Principles of geology.* 3rd. ed. San Francisco: W. H. Freeman and Co.

Hurlbut, C. S. 1971. *Dana's manual of mineralogy.* 18th ed. New York: John Wiley & Sons, Inc.

Leet, L. D., and Judson, S. S. 1971. *Physical geology.* 4th ed. Englewood Cliffs, N.J.: Prentice-Hall, Inc.

Matthews, R. K. 1974. *Dynamic stratigraphy.* Englewood Cliffs, N.J.: Prentice-Hall, Inc.

Press, F., and Siever, R. 1974. *Earth.* San Francisco: W. H. Freeman and Co.

Stokes, W. L. 1966. *Essentials of earth history.* Englewood Cliffs, N.J.: Prentice-Hall, Inc.

4 Nature of Soil and Soil Material

To the soil scientist, particularly the pedologist, the term soil has a specific and ordered meaning. To him soil forms and develops at the earth's surface as a result of the interactions between living and nonliving material. The soil has certain forms and sorts of properties reflecting biogeochemical reactions such as mineral alteration, solution, precipitation, and formation of compounds, among others. The pedologist views the features of the soil in a way that is analogous to a physician viewing anatomy.

Green plants store solar energy by photosynthesis. When plants die, their residues enter the soil and decay. During decomposition of plant residues energy is released and acquires new forms. Of prime importance are the reactions of synthesis in which new mineral and organic substances form. Also many minerals of the soil undergo change and even destruction. For the most part, however, such changes take place at a slow rate. The soil is a dynamic system with biologic and geochemical processes constantly taking place. The rate of biologic reaction is influenced and controlled by changes in temperature, moisture, and other critical factors.

Soil is a three-dimensional body. Soil properties tend to change with depth and accordingly a sample at a depth of three

Figure 4-1   Soil profile showing layering of soil horizons.

inches may have an entirely different appearance and characteristics from that at a depth of twelve or fifteen inches. Thus
when comparative analysis is made between soil adhering to
shoes, clothing, or tires and that from a specific site in nature it is
important not only to consider the location but also the depth
from which the sample was taken. For example, natural soil at
the three-inch depth may be gray in color with 4 percent organic
matter, but at the fifteen-inch depth it may be yellowish brown
color with 1 percent organic matter. The various layers (horizons) of the soil are referred to collectively as the soil profile. Soil
horizons (Fig. 4-1) have their own individual sets of characteristics with respect to appearance, color, texture, and chemical and
mineralogical properties. Differences among horizons can usu-

ally be recognized visually and can be further characterized by laboratory analyses.

Soil Properties

Soil is made up of a mixture of mineral and organic materials. Whereas the organic content varies widely, ranging from less than 1 percent in the deserts to over 90 percent in some bogs, textbooks usually report a value of about 3 percent for the "average" mineral soil. The remaining solid material of the soil is mineral in character. Organic and mineral material collectively make up the solid phase of the soil. Between the solid particles are voids, the volume of which is commonly referred to as pore space; the larger pores are designated as macropores and the smaller ones micropores. The pores are occupied by soil moisture and soil air. The amounts of soil moisture and soil air are dependent on atmospheric conditions and the ratio of the two constantly changes (Fig. 4-2). Thus as water drains from the soil pores, air enters pore space and vice versa.

Under dry conditions life processes are less active but with favorable moisture and temperature biological activity is enhanced. Thus with alternating periods of wetness and dryness coupled with daily soil temperature changes, the biological processes are constantly changing.

The solid phase of the soil offers a better basis for making comparative studies than does the liquid/gaseous phases because of the more permanent nature of the former.

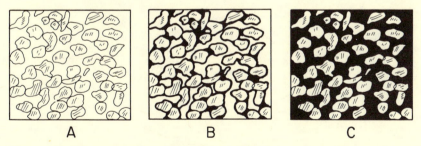

A   B   C

Figure 4-2   Diagrammatic presentation of soil fabric under various moisture levels. *A,* air dry soil; *B,* partially saturated soil; *C,* saturated soil.

Physical Composition of the Soil

About 45 to 60 percent of the soil volume is occupied by soil pores which vary in number, size, and configuration (Fig. 4-3). Usually a cubic foot of soil *in situ* minus water will weigh between 75 and 100 pounds, depending upon the degree of compaction. If a soil is hard, dense, and compact such a condition will indicate a small percentage of soil pores and accordingly the soil will weigh more than 100 pounds per cubic foot. Dense and compact soils have a high *bulk density* or high *volume weight*.

Bulk density is determined by dividing the weight of a water-free soil by its volume, for example, if a cubic foot of soil weighs 87.4 pounds its bulk density would be 1.4 (87.4 divided by the weight of a cubic foot of water which is 62.4 pounds).

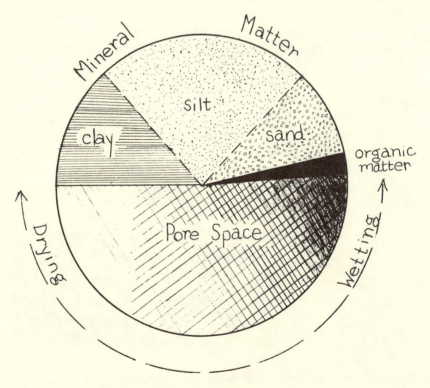

Figure 4-3   Idealized composition of soil.

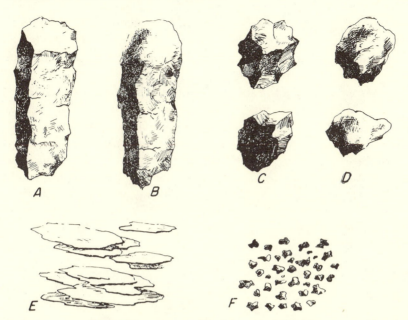

Figure 4-4 Drawings illustrating some of the types of soil structure: *A*, prismatic; *B*, columnar; *C*, angular blocky; *D*, subangular blocky; *E*, platy; and *F*, granular. *Soil Survey Manual*, U.S. Department of Agriculture Handbook No. 18, 1951

Soil structure, which is the arrangement of the soil particles, can be recorded descriptively. Whereas some soils, particularly loose sands, consist of a "structureless" mass, in most soils there is a strong tendency for soil particles to cluster together to form compound structural aggregates. The arrangement of the aggregates plus their size and shape make up the *soil structure* (Fig. 4-4). Soil structure is one of the more important of soil properties, but on the other hand it is generally one of the more tenuous criteria for use in forensic science. The forensic scientist, by necessity, usually has to work with small quantities of material such as splashes of mud and scrapings from shoes or fenders under which cases the aggregates, if once present, usually have been altered. Once structural aggregates are removed from their original position they tend to crumble, slake, and lose their original form. When possible it is important, however, for a portion of the sample to be reserved for structural examination. In cases of disturbed sites such as fill areas and gravel pits, compound soil structure seldom exists except possibly in some organic-enriched forms near the surface of the soil.

Particle sizes of the soil minerals are classed as sand, silt, and clay. This is solely a physical measurement and the terms, therefore, have little relation to chemical or mineral composition. Various disciplines such as geology, engineering, and pedology may use somewhat different measurements and terms, but the principle is largely the same. The percentages of sand, silt, and clay form a textural grouping or *soil class* such as

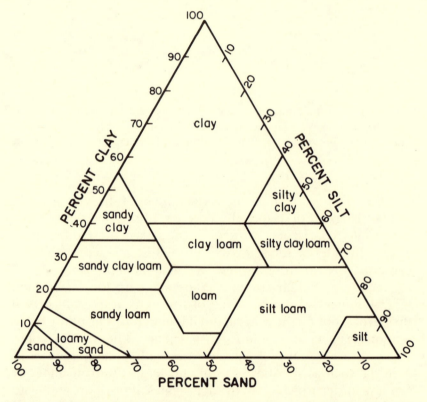

Figure 4-5 Chart showing the percentages of clay (below 0.002 mm.), silt (0.002 to 0.05 mm.), and sand (0.05 to 2.0 mm.) in the basic soil textural classes.

loam, silt loam, loamy sand, and others (Fig. 4-5). Where there are large amounts of gravel or stones present such terms are added to the soil textural name, for example, stony loam.

Chemical Composition of Soils

Soil chemistry, a large and complex field, can be used effectively as a fundamental forensic avenue. Unfortunately, selective chemical data also can be used as a kind of gamemanship. There is an infinite number of determinations, combinations, and ratios that can be concocted from chemical determinations, and therefore it is important that the scientist have the wisdom of Solomon rather than the dexterity of Houdini.

Soil chemical composition will, in some situations, and with some methods of analyses, show little local variation from one site to another, whereas in other cases using other kinds of analysis changes may occur over very short distances.

Total Chemical Composition of the Major Constituents

Total soil chemical composition has been used to some extent in forensic science and in general it can be stated that it has met with mixed success. One of the procedures has been to have a chemist "analyze" soil samples. This often means determination of some major constituents such as silica, iron, aluminum, and perhaps others such as the trace elements, that is, those that occur in relatively small amounts. In order to give some idea of the general composition of soils Table 4-1 lists data for major soil constituents from selected areas. SiO_2 usually comprises up to 75 percent of the soil and in sandy soils values will be higher. $Fe_2O_3 + Al_2O_3$ collectively make up about 5 to 15 percent (Tab. 4-1) of the soil. So these three compounds (silica, iron, and alumina) will generally account for 80 to 90 percent of the total soil. In the humid tropics soils have been leached of much of their silica so that the SiO_2 content will be much lower and also because of the low solubility of iron and alumina, these latter elements will be higher than in cooler climates. It will be

Table 4-1   CHEMICAL COMPOSITION OF SOILS
(Marbut, 1935)

	Chester Loam (Virginia) %	Marshall Silt Loam (Iowa) %	Gray Silt Loam (Nevada) %
SiO_2	75.2	72.6	61.7
Al_2O_3	11.1	12.0	13.8
Fe_2O_3	4.2	3.1	3.9
CaO	0.2	0.8	5.5
MgO	0.5	0.8	2.6
Na_2O	0.9	1.4	1.5
K_2O	2.2	2.2	2.9
MnO	0.1	0.1	0.1
TiO_2	1.4	0.6	0.5
P_2O_5	0.1	0.1	0.1
SO_3	0.1	0.1	0.1
Ig. loss	3.8	6.0	7.6

noted that the compounds listed in Table 4-1 are almost entirely expressed as oxides,* for example, silicon dioxide (SiO_2), calcium oxide (CaO), etc.

Only in certain cases will values determined for the elements silicon, iron, aluminum, potassium, calcium, magnesium, and sodium in a soil give a strong indication as to origin of the sample. There are special situations, however, in which certain elements could be used as tracers, such as titanium, which is commonly in the form of the mineral ilmenite, or in the case of soils forming or ores high in chromium, nickel or manganese. Limestone soils containing native particles of calcite or dolomite would also serve as good examples of tracers. Such information would be far more convincing than would showing that two samples had about equal amounts of silica or alumina.

* Association of Official Agricultural Chemists. *Official and Tentative Methods of Analysis,* Washington, D.C. (various editions). [Now Association of Official Analytical Chemists, Box 540, Benjamin Franklin Station, Washington, D.C.]

If one chooses to make a comparative analysis, should the total soil (that is, all material smaller than 2 mm) be analyzed or simply those particles within one size-range be used? Data derived from the total soil will show a different set of values than those from specific size fractions. If the finer material is selected the SiO_2 values will decrease, while those for Al_2O_3 and Fe_2O_3 will increase (Fig. 4-6).

Total Chemical Composition of the Trace Constituents

Trace elements in soils offer some forensic possibilities, especially if there are concentrations of certain elements present. Chemistry of the trace elements, however, is not as clearly defined as is the case with the major soil constituents. Table 4-2 lists some trace elements present in soil and soil clay, the content of which usually ranges up to several hundred ppm or even

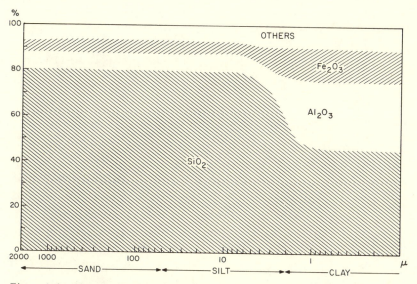

Figure 4-6 Chemical composition of soils and sediments tends to vary according to the size of the various fractions. The finer material usually contains larger percentages of Fe_2O_3 and Al_2O_3 but smaller percentages of SiO_2. The critical size range where such changes take place is 1–5 microns.

Table 4-2   TRACE ELEMENT COMPOSITION OF SOIL AND
SOIL CLAY
(Connor, Shimp and Tedrow, 1957)

	Cu ppm	Mn ppm	Zn ppm	Ni ppm	Co ppm	Sn ppm	Pb ppm	Cr ppm	V ppm	Ga ppm
A horizon of a soil formed on Silurian quartzite										
Total Soil	4	20	16	3	ND *	5	8	17	11	2
Soil Clay	135	80	98	15	ND	20	44	101	133	27
A horizon of a soil formed on carbonate drift										
Total Soil	13	121	169	18	3	2	138	22	56	8
Soil Clay	56	156	318	45	9	1	30	83	119	28

* ND not determined.

higher. There is generally a concentration of trace elements in the clay fractions of soils, and therefore if any comparison is made between various samples it is important to make comparison within the same size-range of soil particles.

Near smelters and certain manufacturing areas the concentration of certain trace elements increases. For example, the topsoil near a zinc smelter in an Eastern town was found to have nearly 6 percent zinc.

Soil Varieties

How many varieties of soil exist? It would be misleading to state that there is any specific number of soils. There is as yet no one detailed international system of soil taxonomy which has been accepted universally such as those of the plant, animal, and mineral kingdoms. Most soil scientists would agree that no two points on the surface of the globe would have precisely the same soil. In 1675 in England, John Evelyn, reflecting philosophical discussions of his day, stated that there were at least 179,001,060 different "sorts of earths." In 1909 the U.S. Department of Agriculture listed 230 soil series in the United States which were further divided into soil types; for example, Hagerstown (a deep well-drained soil formed in the limestone valleys of eastern United States) is a soil series name, whereas Hagerstown clay loam and Hagerstown silt loam are soil types. In 1930 in the United States there were approximately 1500 soil series recognized and by 1965 the list had grown to 10,466. Thus the number of recognized soils in any one area is largely a response to purpose, need, and intensity of the survey. If all of the soils in the United States were mapped on a scale of four inches per mile—a scale that is now generally used by the U.S. Department of Agriculture—there probably would be some 50,000 varieties recognized. Even with this large number there would still be variations found within the mapped soil units.

Study of soils has often been used on a regional scale to assist an investigation. In the well-known Coors kidnap and murder case the victim disappeared one morning near Morrison, Colorado, a town southwest of Denver in the foothills of the Rocky Mountains. His automobile was found with the motor still running. His glasses and splotches of blood were observed at the scene. However, there was no indication of his fate or location. One month later a suspect vehicle was found burning on a dump in Atlantic City, New Jersey. Soil samples taken from under the fender of this vehicle showed four layers. The outermost and thus the last deposed layer compared with soil samples collected at the entrance to the dump. The three inner layers contained mineral grains characteristic of the Rocky Mountain front area near Denver. Apparently the car had been driven only on pavement across the country and thus had failed to pick up recognizable soil layers between Colorado and New Jersey. Over 360 soil samples were collected from the Rocky Mountain front area west of Denver in an effort to compare these samples with those found on the burnt automobile. This was an effort to locate the general area where the victim might be found. While this study was in progress the body of the victim was found by hunters twenty-seven miles south of Denver. Additional study revealed that the second youngest layer of soil from the suspect automobile compared with the scene where the victim was found and the third layer compared with soil samples taken from the victim's ranch. The fourth and oldest layer was not comparable with any of the 421 soil samples collected and studied in this case, but probably came from the Denver area. This evidence contributed to a conviction for kidnapping and murder because it was possible to relate the suspect to the burnt automobile.

Local Variations

In the case of stolen tobacco that was later sold to a warehouse, sufficient soil from the tobacco field had collected on the leaves to permit a study of this soil and samples collected from the fields of the original owner. It was possible to determine that the stolen tobacco had grown in the southern half of one of the original owner's ten-acre fields. In addition, study of the soil material taken from the leaves of the stolen tobacco were studied along with soil samples taken from fields owned by the suspects. These samples did not compare and their alibi, that it was their own tobacco, was not supported.

Uniformity of soil properties horizontally is of critical importance, because the question may arise as to how far from the sampling site a set of soil data can be extrapolated radially 10 feet — 100 yards — 1 mile. In answering such a question there are at least two main facets to be considered: (1) possible changes in lithology (geologic-induced changes), and (2) changes induced by shallowness, and wetness (pedologic changes). Locally, there may be high order changes of material within short distances such as those found along certain stream and glacial deposits. Therefore, data derived from any one location cannot in all situations be extrapolated far from the sampling site. Even with fairly uniform geologic conditions there is a tendency for certain soil properties to change within short distances due to depressions, shallow rocky sectors, and related factors. Figure 4-7 shows an idealized cross section with four major varieties being present. The shallow terrestric soils (A) are usually, but not always, found on the steep terrain, the deep well-drained soils (B) are found on sloping to level terrain, the wet mineral soils (C) tend to be present in depressions and in the very wet swampy sectors, peat or muck (D) may be present. Whereas the mineral soils (A, B and C) may have certain properties in common such as the percentage of iron or silica, or the percentage of

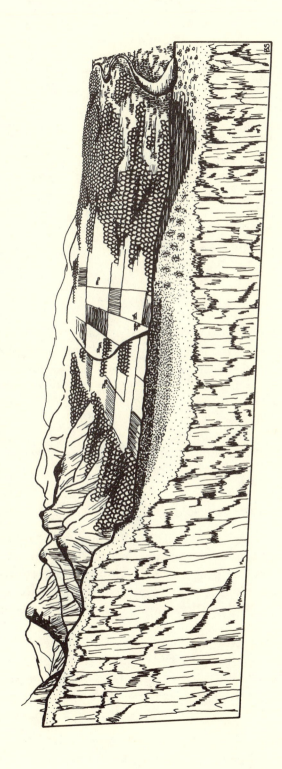

A   B   C   D

Figure 4-7   Idealized diagram showing local soil changes: *A*, shallow soil; *B*, deep, well-drained soil; *C*, wet mineral soil; *D*, peat and muck.

quartz and feldspar, there are differences among the soils such
as appearance, color, and organic matter content. The soils
shown diagrammatically (Fig. 4-7) have their own discrete properties, and if one is fortunate enough to obtain a sample of
soil—preferably a "clod" measuring one-half inch or more from
a suspect's shoes or automobile it is possible to make some
projections as to possible origin of the material. Samples from
Figure 4-7(A and B) will generally show more uniform colors of
browns, yellows, and grays, whereas those from the wet sites will
show dull gray colors, often with a speckled (mottled) appearance (Fig. 4-7[C]). Figure 4-8 shows a natural soil from a well-
drained site with distinct layers (horizons). Color within the
individual horizons is uniform and shows a high degree of
oxidation. In depressed sites nearby, however, due to prolonged
periods of water saturation, the soil has taken on a mottled
appearance of grays and rusty colored spots.

Whereas the chemical or mineralogical characteristics of the
mineral material are emphasized, the organic material on the
surface of the soil, including both living and dead plant parts,
may be equally important in making projections as to origin of
the sample. Leaves, grasses, twigs, roots, and other plant parts
such as seed pods, even if partially decomposed, can usually be
identified by trained personnel, and from such analyses projections can be made as to possible origin.

Soil Properties in Various Climatic Zones

Apart from variations in soils locally, there are also major
differences in soils present in various climatic zones. Thus, if one
compares soil from the forests of northeastern United States to
the deserts of Utah or Arizona, major differences would be
found. The "black" soils of the Midwest, the "gray" soils of the
deserts and the "red" soils of the tropics have attracted the
attention of travelers and explorers since early times. Nearly a
century ago, a Russian, V. V. Dokuchaev stated that soil is a
function of parent material, relief, climate, biotic factors, and
time. This statement has stood the test of the years.

Figure 4-8   A soil profile in southern New Jersey showing 4 distinct layers (horizons). The surface consists of a 1-inch layer of organic litter. The upper mineral layer is composed of a gray sand (A Horizon). Beginning at the top of the shovel handle and continuing to the shank of the shovel the soil is a yellowish brown, iron-stained sand (B Horizon). The blade of the shovel rests against a yellowish gray sand (C Horizon). The various soil layers develop from leaching, translocation, and other processes within the soil.

Disturbed vs. Undisturbed Sites

The problem occasionally arises as to locating disturbed areas such as burial sites or excavations. Such situations exist not only in forensic science, but also in the military in connection with the burial of land mines and booby traps. In the battle of the Monongahela in 1755, General Braddock was mortally wounded and his body supposedly buried by his comrades in the roadbed used by the retreating wagon trains. Apparently the British troops believed this was the best method of concealing the burial site. His body was never recovered. In some cases, soil features can be used as a reliable index in locating disturbed conditions, but in others the technique would be tenuous and doubtful. If we consider a situation in which the soil has developed specific layers (horizons) as shown in Figure 4-8, it is impossible to excavate such a site and restore the soil layers to their original state. During the digging and subsequent replacement of the soil to the excavation, organic layers become buried and there is a general derangement, and mixing of the original layers. The minute details of the original features are destroyed or altered so that changes can be detected. One of the important preliminaries in locating a disturbed site should be the examination of the organic matter covering the soil. In a forested area, the organic covering shows a layering effect with the surface debris consisting of a one- to two-inch layer of leaves and twigs which have undergone little or no decomposition. But underneath the leaves the organic matter has decomposed to a greasy or mealy organic humic-like substance. Examination of the "layering effect" of the organic matter in a wooded area generally gives a clue to possible site disturbance. After a site is once disturbed, how long will it take for conditions to return to their original state? Humus forms may in some cases regenerate to their original state in a matter of years, with each site having its own set of properties, but setting an absolute value in terms of years for humus regeneration is rather nebulous.

There is a variety of additional techniques available for the location of bodies in soil. Nonembalmed bodies have been located using instruments that detect the methane gas given off by the decomposing body. Five-foot metal rods are forced into the ground, removed, and the probe of a methane detector inserted. If the soil contains large amounts of naturally decomposing organic matter the methane produced by this material will be recorded and the additional methane produced by a body may not be sufficient to be detected.

In forensic studies there is a natural tendency to focus on

the mineral portion of the soil but the character of the soil organic matter should not be discounted. A close relationship exists between soils and vegetation and from the character of organic matter alone one can make some projections as to possible origin of the organic material. The character of the humus layer itself can also be used as an important criterion. In broadest terms, the organic matter in forested areas acquires a set of properties reflecting the environment. Under conifer vegetation the organic matter is deficient in calcium, potassium and other important bases resulting in an acid condition which is an unfavorable environment for biological breakdown. The humus, therefore, builds up in layered form, described as a *raw humus* or *mor*. Under hardwoods with a good supply of bases, biological activity is enhanced and the organic material is broken down and incorporated into the upper mineral horizon referred to as a *mull*. In situations where there is an intermediate degree of organic breakdown the organic material is designated as a *moder*. Botanists can generally identify some of the plant parts in the organic matter at the surface of the soil.

Peat and Muck

In low areas where the soil is saturated with water most of the year, peat-like material accumulates. Whereas all peaty material appears to be monotonously similar, in detail there may be considerable variation among samples. Peaty material in some sites will be only a foot or so deep, but in other extremes it will be as much as 100 feet deep. Fiberous organic material in the wet sites is generally considered to be peat, but with partial decomposition of the organic material to a homogeneous mass the material is more correctly termed muck. Appearance alone gives some indication of the type of place where a sample originally formed. The following factors should be considered in determining the origin of the peat:

1. *Appearance.* Peat forms from many types of vegetation but the original plant parts can generally be identified. If conditions necessitate detailed information the peat can be thinsectioned. This is accomplished by drying the peat, impregnat-

ing it with plastic, sawing the plastic-encased material into thin sections, mounting the sections on a glass slide and examining them with a microscope.

2. *Chemical composition.* Chemical composition of peats varies but a total elemental analysis itself may not in itself be very indicative of origin. The carbon content of dried high-grade peat approximates 50 percent and there is usually less than 1 percent of potassium, calcium, and magnesium present. Under most situations it can be readily determined whether a peat formed under coastal conditions. Peats which form along the coastal marshes have distinctive properties in that they are subject to inundation by tidal flow and commonly contain salt. The degree of salinity can readily be determined by electrical conductivity measurements. This is a simple procedure which can be carried out in a chemical laboratory.

Pollen

Techniques using pollen and spores in the soil offer some possibilities in forensic science. These relatively new techniques, often referred to as *palynology* (from the Greek meaning to sprinkle with fine dust), can, under certain situations, be used in making projections as to where a sample came from. Pollen grains are produced in the anthers of flowers during bloom. Some plants produce great quantities of pollen; for example, a tassel of corn may produce as many as 50,000,000 pollen grains. While pollen tends to be dispersed over wide areas—often hundreds of miles—the types and amount of pollen in any one soil sample may be characteristic and localized. This is especially true for the larger pollen such as cactus. Hay-fever sufferers are well aware when they get into a "ragweed patch" during the pollen season. In most instances, pollen is easily identified by microscopic techniques (Fig. 4-9). Although studies will give information as to whether the pollen is from ragweed, corn, or oak, it cannot be used as a complete key. For example, all grass pollen looks alike except for size. Size of pollen grains varies greatly, but most pollen grains approximate 20 to 60 microns.

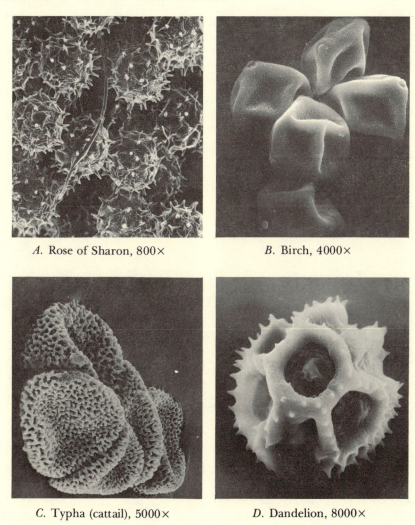

A. Rose of Sharon, 800×   *B.* Birch, 4000×

C. Typha (cattail), 5000×   *D.* Dandelion, 8000×

Figure 4-9 Scanning electron micrographs of pollen grains.

References

Bridges, E. M. 1970. *World soils.* London: Cambridge Univ. Press.
Connor, J., Shimp, N. F., and Tedrow, J. F. C. 1957. A spectrographic study of trace elements in some podzolic soils. *Soil Sci.* 83:65–73.

Marbut, C. F. 1935. *Atlas of American agriculture*, Part III. Washington, D.C.: U.S. Govt. Prtg. Office.

Robinson, G. W. 1949. *Soils: their origin, constitution and classification.* London: T. Murby.

U.S. Department of Agriculture. 1951. *Soil survey manual.* (USDA Handbook No. 18.) Washington, D.C.: U.S. Govt. Prtg. Office.

Wilde, S. A. 1971. Forest humus: its classification on a genetic basis. *Soil Sci.* 111:1–2.

Wodehouse, R. P. 1959. *Pollen grains.* New York: Hafner Publishing Co.

5 Commercial and Artificial Earth Materials

Rocks and minerals are used by man in a wide variety of industrial and commercial ways. In addition, artificial minerals and mineral products such as glass and abrasives are often manufactured and widely distributed. In these commercial products minerals and rocks are often mixed together with other materials or new materials are created to produce a highly distinctive substance that can have important evidential value. This is particularly true in urban areas where the products of man are concentrated. Indeed, these products are commonly found as particles in the otherwise natural soils within our cities.

The identification of these materials is normally made in the same ways as that of natural materials. However, the recognition that the substance being studied is an artificial or commercial product is often of value in itself for forensic purposes. For example, the presence of recognized safe insulation material on a person when the person is not in the safe-building or the repair business raises serious questions as to the source of a material that is normally found encased in steel and liberated only after blowing, breaking, cutting, or drilling a safe.

The purpose of this chapter is to discuss briefly some of the more common commercial or artificial earth materials that have been used for forensic purposes. It should be pointed out that the composition of many manufactured products are trade secrets of the manufacturer. Composition of such materials is usually known, however, by certain forensic laboratories. Even when a material may not be identified directly as coming from a specific product, the methods of comparison that are applicable to other earth materials may be used whenever a sample of the material is available for control.

Glass

Glass is an extremely common material as physical evidence. Broken automobile headlights, windows broken while entering a building, broken bottles used as weapons, glass beads used in projection screens, and highway center strip reflectors—the list is almost endless. In many cases two or more different glasses have been found on suspects which compare with glass from windows broken during an illegal entry. When such multiple comparisons are made the evidential value becomes even stronger than a single comparison. This, of course, can only be done by careful sampling at the scene and from the suspect's person or property.

Glass is composed primarily of calcium, sodium, and silica with minor amounts of other elements and may be natural, as in the case of volcanic glass (obsidian) or artificial man-made glasses. The latter is manufactured by melting sand and other rocks and quickly cooling the liquid. Glass is isotropic and thus has only one refractive index. Under the polarizing microscope it will remain at extinction and thus stay black when the microscope stage is rotated with crossed polars. Quartz, which is uniaxial, can be distinguished from glass using the petrographic microscope because quartz will go to extinction at only four positions during one full rotation of the microscope stage.

The comparison of glass-like objects requires that there be large variation in the properties of glasses so that when two pieces of glass are measured there is a very high probability that similarity of properties means that they came from the same source. Glass produced prior to World War II had far more variation in composition from batch to batch and from different parts of the same batch than glass produced today. However, it is equally important in the study of glass that the natural variation in properties within a single pane or headlamp be known. This is true because two parts of the same piece of glass will not have identical properties. *Refractive index* and *dispersion,* that is, the refractive index difference measured at two different wave lengths or colors of light, are the two optical properties commonly measured in attempting to compare glass. Specific gravity is also a valuable property. Chemical analyses have limited use with common glasses but have proved useful in the study and identification of special glass such as colored glass, opal glass, soft, low-melting glass, and crown glass.

Safe Insulation

There are two general types of safes in use in the United States: the fire-resistant safe which has two or more inches of insulation between its walls and the burglar-resistant safe composed entirely of metal (often encased in concrete or placed inside a fire-resistant vault or inside a larger fire-resistant safe). Because the insulation in fire-resistant safes is often porous and relatively soft, it is commonly found on the clothing and tools of the safe burglar, in his toolbox, or in a vehicle (Fig. 5-1).

Numerous types of materials have been used as safe insulation including gypsum and cork, dolomite and cement, cinders, gypsum with asbestos, gypsum with wood chips, corrugated asbestos, gypsum and/or calcium carbonate with diatomaceous earth, and even ordinary mud or cement.

The three types described below include the majority of safe insulations encountered in the forensic laboratory:

1. Modern safes made by some of the leading manufacturers contain a mixture of Portland cement, vermiculite mica and diatomaceous earth (Fig. 5-2). The diatoms are usually observed on a glass slide by transmitted light at about 360× magnification after dissolving away the cement in hydrochloric acid. Some safe insulations contain fresh-water diatoms; some salt-water diatoms. These are usually seen as sintered fragments and

Figure 5-1   Safe that has been opened by ripping. Note the chunks of insulation and powdered insulation on the floor, safe, and furniture. *Courtesy of Piscataway, N.J., Police Department*

are usually associated with sponge spicules; they are, however, easily identified as to class by the forensic microscopist. If the three above materials are identified together, the experienced laboratory examiner can conclude positively that even a tiny lump of the material is safe insulation to the exclusion of other sources of similar materials.

2. Many older safes, made before 1936, contain natural cement as insulation. Natural cement is a product resulting from the calcining of certain argillaceous limestones. The argillaceous material is usually shale, which is easily observed under the low-power microscope and which varies among safes in colors, particle size, and abundance. Some natural cement was made by burning limestone and coal or coke in a kiln. Insulations made from this product will contain coal particles and cinders. The

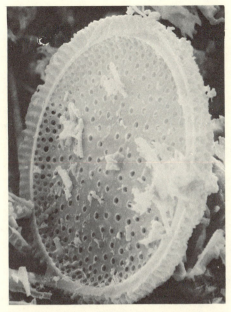

6000×

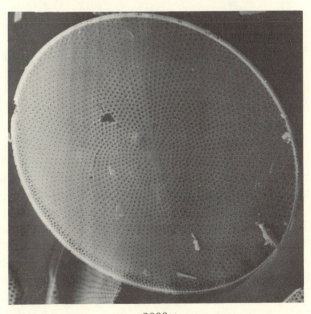

2000×

Figure 5-2   Two of the many kinds of diatoms that make up diatomaceous earth. *Courtesy of Robert Holzer*

87

forensic microscopist can identify this insulation and, since there is no record of its being used without sand or gravel except in safes, he can conclude positively that even a small lump of the neat natural cement is insulation from an older safe.

3. Some modern light-weight safes use a very porous mixture of Portland cement and vermiculite. One large company, under several brand names, produces safes using an insulation composed of gypsum and sawdust; another uses gypsum alone.

By experience and maintaining files of various insulations encountered, the forensic microscopist can learn to identify many safes by examination of the insulation alone. Because of variations between insulations, comparisons between safe insulation from a crime scene with that on a suspect's belongings are always of value.

In a classic case the suspect was thought to have a bad case of dandruff because his hair contained numerous small white specks. Close examination of these specks with a powerful microscope revealed that they were diatoms. Diatoms are the microscopic organisms and a very large number of fossil species exist. In a sample collected from the suspect's hair thirteen distinct species of diatoms were identified. Study of the insulation of a safe that had been recently entered revealed that it was made of diatomaceous earth and that the same thirteen species of diatoms comprised the insulation. This evidence led to his arrest and subsequently he was convicted of the crime. Diatomaceous earth, sometimes known as *Kieselguhr* or *infusorial earth* can yield much information of evidential value because of the diversity of diatoms found in most deposits.

Asbestos is the fibrous variety of several of the amphibole minerals or more commonly the fibrous serpentine mineral chrysotile (Fig. 5-3). It comes in a wide variety of kinds that are easily distinguishable. These insulation materials differ from manufacturer to manufacturer and may be changed from time to time as a better product is found or a source of material changes. In most cases it is possible to use the standard methods of comparison where samples have been obtained from broken safes. An interesting example of this type of comparison involved the entering and breaking into of two safes in a small

Figure 5-3   Asbestos fibers at high magnification.

town in southern Maryland. One safe was located in a movie theater and the other in a nearby restaurant. Two suspects were apprehended shortly after the restaurant crime. One admitted to the crime and stated that the other was completely innocent. However, in the trouser cuffs of the second, the apparently innocent suspect, were particles of a cement-type safe insulation that compared with the insulation from the broken safe in the restaurant. In addition, particles of a vermiculite mica safe insulation were found in the suspect's automobile and these compared with the insulation found in the broken safe from the theater.

Building Materials

Bricks, concrete blocks, plaster, cement, ceramic materials, etc., all offer the possibility of having important evidential value when identified or studied by the various comparison methods. These materials commonly adhere to clothing or tools during forceable entries. They also become embedded in the fenders and frames of automobiles during impact (Fig. 5-4). Because construction materials are commonly made of mineral materials and commonly represent the combination of a variety of minerals or rocks at a specific time for a specific purpose they can be highly distinctive (Fig. 5-5).

The office of a national organization was illegally entered in a town in eastern Idaho. The safe in this office was blown using nitroglycerine, and the contents, amounting to several hundred dollars, were removed. Entry was made by removing a part of the brick and plaster from the wall. In a nearby hotel room particles of brick and plaster that compared with those collected from the scene of the crime were found, suggesting that the former occupant should be considered a suspect. The suspect

Figure 5-4   Left, dent in the fender of a vehicle that hit a concrete post; *right,* particles of concrete imbedded in the impression. *Courtesy of Piscataway, N.J., Police Department*

Figure 5-5 Concrete seen in thin section. The kinds of rocks and minerals include varieties of basalt (trap rock), limestone, and quartzite.

was apprehended in another city while "casing" another office of the same organization.

Plaster is produced by heating the mineral gypsum ($CaSO_4 \cdot 2H_2O$) to slightly over 100° C., thus driving off part of the water contained in the mineral. When water is added to the plaster new crystals of gypsum form, thus setting or turning the material from a powder to a rock-like material used in wallboard, safe insulation or other building materials. Most plaster and cement contain rock and mineral particles whose identification contributes to the study of these materials. If this material is to be collected and studied for forensic purposes it is very important that it be placed in an air-tight container and not heated again, thus preventing the conversion of all or part of the gypsum back to the plaster or low-water form. If these changes on heating were to occur then positive comparison would be impossible. Indeed, such heating produced accidentally in the preparation of the thin section could represent a destruction of the evidence.

Cleaning and Face Powders

These commercial powders commonly have a mineral base or mineral filler. The specific minerals used tend to differ from one product to another and manufacturers tend to change the size and composition of minerals through time (Fig. 5-6). Thus, these materials can be studied for comparison or lack of comparison. In the case of a young man who assaulted a young lady by kicking her in the face, the identification of powder on the toe of his shoe and the comparison of that powder with a sample of her face powder proved convincing. The face powder had a titanium oxide base in the form of the mineral anatase. This was identified by X-ray diffraction analysis. It is interesting to note that a chemical analysis would have detected the titanium but that better evidence was provided by identifying the specific titanium mineral. The soft mineral talc forms the base of most talcum or dusting powders. These powders tend to vary from product to product in particle size; some are ground finer than others. They also differ in the associated minerals that are found

Figure 5-6 Left, cleaning powder (1000×), and *right,* talcum powder (2000×), under the scanning electron microscope. *Courtesy of Robert Holzer*

with the talc. Different manufacturers commonly obtain their talc from different mines, providing thus the possibility of different minerals associated with the talc. In addition, the sources for an individual manufacturer change with time, producing considerable variations in the products. For example, since 1972, cornstarch has seen increased use.

Abrasives

Abrasive materials may be natural such as *emery,* a mixture of the minerals corundum and magnetite, hematite, or iron spinel; or artificial such as Carborundum and Alundum. Natural diamond, garnet and various forms of quartz are also used in some applications. These materials offer the possibility of study and have many forensic applications. Natural materials tend to be more diverse than artificial materials. Abrasives have been used as evidence in cases involving malicious damage and sabotage where the abrasive has been introduced into machinery causing damage to the working parts. Grinding wheels, used to remove serial numbers or open safes, sometimes leave particles of grit that offer the possibility of comparison with grinding wheels found associated with suspects.

Commercial Sands

There is a wide variety of sands used for commercial purposes. These vary from ordinary quartz sand sold as it comes from the sand pit for such purposes as concrete aggregate, to a variety of special sands that may be treated to remove certain sizes of particles or minerals or are blended with other sources to produce a product for manufacture of glass, oil well treatment, sand boxes, molding forms used in foundries, etc. These materials can be useful for identification and studied for possible comparison with control samples. In a case of breaking and entering of a foundry in Toronto, Canada, the shoes of the suspect contained abundant grains of the mineral olivine. This mineral does not exist naturally in the soils of Toronto area. It is, however, imported as a special molding sand for use by three foundries in the area and some had been spilled outside the window that had been used for the entry. The suspect denied having ever been at any of the foundries. The olivine sand from the suspect's shoes was found to compare with the sand collected from outside the entry window. The mineralogical comparison combined with the known distribution of potentially similar material provided the scientist with the opportunity to state that there was a very high probability that the two samples were from the same spot and thus the subject had with an equally high probability been at the scene.

References

Coes, L. 1971. *Abrasives.* New York: Springer-Verlag.

Walls, H. J. 1968. *Forensic science.* New York: F. A. Praeger Co.

Winchell, A. N. 1931. *The microscopic characters of artificial inorganic solid substances or artificial minerals.* 2nd ed. New York: John Wiley & Sons.

6 The Problems of Sampling

All laboratory studies of earth materials—soils, rocks, minerals and fossils—involve the examination of samples, that is, a relatively small part of a larger mass of material. When a geologist studies an area where valuable minerals have been found or are suspected he collects samples of the minerals and rocks. These rocks and minerals are collected in such a way as to insure that they are representative of the ore and the rock. This procedure is necessary so that information about the value of the ore found in the samples can be used to evaluate and predict the total value of the whole body of ore. It is not possible to sample the entire ore body because if this were done the ore body would already have been removed and a scientific prediction of what might be found and its value would be unnecessary.

In most forensic applications of soil studies we are faced with two separate types of sampling problems. The first, over which we have little control, is the sample or samples directly associated with the crime or incident. These samples may take many forms, such as lumps of soil on a highway at the scene of an accident, soil on shoes or clothing, safe insulation, dust in hair, microscopic marine or fresh-water animals in the lungs of a drowning victim, rocks or glass used as weapons, abrasives in

machinery, etc. The second type of sample, which the investigator or the forensic geologist can select, is the control material.
These are samples taken for comparison with samples associated
with the crime or incident. Such samples may include soil removed from the frame and fenders of a suspect vehicle, soil
samples from the scene of the crime, insulation samples from the
victim's safe, water samples with their contained microscopic
animals and plants from suspected areas of drowning, rocks or
glass from known locations that might have been the source of
the weapon, sources of abrasives, etc.

The Associated or Questioned Samples

These samples are taken many times by accident and almost
never with any attempt to provide a sample that is representative
of the materials from which it was derived. For example, a rapist
normally makes no deliberate attempt to fill the cuffs of his
trousers with a sample of soil that is truly representative of the
sizes of particles present at the scene of the incident. Thus the
sample collected in the trouser cuffs may lack some of the larger
particles present at the scene. In this sense the sample in the
cuffs probably can never be expected to be exactly the same as
the sample or samples collected for control that includes all the
available sizes. In such cases the only proper study that can be
attempted must be made on the particles in the control samples
that are of the same sizes present in the crime-associated samples. In the case of forceable breaking and entering the earth
materials collected on entry tools or clothing which may include
roofing granules, masonry, brick, rock, etc., may not be truly
representative samples. The materials collected by a person
during such an incident may in part represent those grains that
are loose or most easily broken. Thus it is unlikely that the
sample can be the same as a bulk sample of the original materials.
In such cases professional judgment may be used in choosing the
methods of analysis in order to establish comparison or lack of
comparison. The competent professional can make such judgments while the incompetent will blindly attempt to process the
bulk samples without judgment.

A second type of sampling for most associated or questioned material involves the forensic geologist when he removes earth material from the shoe, clothing, vehicle, shipping box, etc. This can be done by a number of methods. Where a lump of soil is involved it should be collected and preserved intact. Preservation of the original sample is especially important when layers of material are involved, such as a lump of soil from underneath the fender of a vehicle. Such samples permit the study of the *stratigraphy,* that is, the particles of the individual layers from oldest to youngest. From such samples it is also possible to see how the particles which make up the lump fit together. Normally samples at this stage are collected from a person's clothing by shaking them over a clean sheet of paper and carefully collecting individual samples. In some cases a vacuum cleaner has been used, but must be handled with caution, using a clean collecting bag. This method is generally unsatisfactory because the lumps of soil are broken and the physical appearance of some of the particles may be changed. The method of Max Frei-Sulzer of the Zurich police has received much attention. In 1951 he began using Scotch adhesive tape for the collection and preservation of small samples. This method is generally unsatisfactory because the adhesive on the tape may interfere with many analyses and because of the difficulty in removing particles from the tape.

The Control Samples

Control geologic samples are of two types, those collected from a crime scene or alibi location (Fig. 6-1) and those that exist in museums or collections as part of the scientist's normal professional resources. Those from the crime scene or alibi location that are needed for the purpose of study in an individual case may be collected in at least two possible ways. The most common method is for the investigator to collect samples as part of the investigation and submit them with other items of physical evidence to the laboratory. When this is done the responsibility for proper sampling lies with the investigator and the procedure followed is normally determined by the forensic laboratory.

Suggested procedures are normally published in an instruction manual for investigators prepared by the laboratory. These are made available by most laboratories to their potential clients. In the case of materials from vehicles, separate samples, each preserving intact lumps of soil, should be taken from under all four fenders. Oil or grease with contained minerals, rocks, and related material should be sampled from several places under a vehicle when these samples are to be studied in conjunction with similar material left at the scene in accident cases (Fig. 6-2). Such samples should be carefully labeled showing the location where the sample was taken. Where the crime scene involves a vertical cut into the earth such as a quarry or grave, samples should be taken from each bed, layer, or horizon that exhibits a difference in color, texture, or mineralogy to the eye. Where glass, building, or synthetic material is concerned, the sample should be pure, sufficient for analysis, and representative. If two or more different pieces of broken glass are present they should be sampled separately.

Samples obtained from museums or collections that are a

Figure 6-1 Collecting of soil samples that fell from under the fender of a vehicle at the scene of a hit-and-run accident. *Courtesy of Piscataway, N.J., Police Department*

Figure 6-2   Suspension of a vehicle showing a place where the head of a victim in a hit-and-run accident removed grease which contained mineral material. A sample was collected from the head of the victim and from the vehicle in the area of impact. *Courtesy of Piscataway, N.J., Police Department*

normal part of the scientist's professional resources are many and varied. He may use fossils or minerals that have been collected and identified in the past for comparison with samples that come to his attention in the course of a study. This comparison may provide him with a correct identification of the material and in some cases a locality where similar material could have been obtained. A geologic map (Fig. 6-3) showing the distribution on the surface of the earth of the kinds of rocks that are found at various places may prove invaluable in determining the possible source of rocks and soils. In a case of assault and vandalism where the victims were injured by hurled rocks, the rocks recovered at the scene were angular blocks of an unusual igneous rock type that existed in a relatively small area in the southern part of the United States. Study of geologic maps indicated that the nearest outcrop of this rock type was twenty

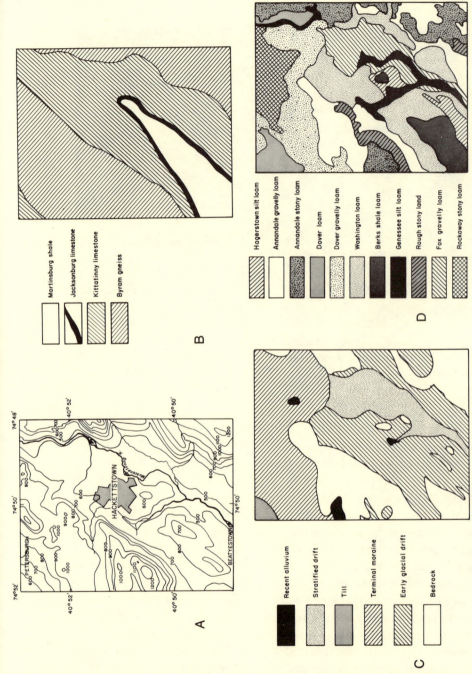

Figure 6-3 Geologic maps. *A*, topographical map; *B*, bedrock geologic map; *C*, surficial geologic map; *D*, soil map.

B

- Martinsburg shale
- Jacksonburg limestone
- Kittatinny limestone
- Byram gneiss

D

- Hagerstown silt loam
- Annandale gravelly loam
- Annandale stony loam
- Dover loam
- Dover gravelly loam
- Washington loam
- Berks shale loam
- Genessee silt loam
- Rough stony land
- Fox gravelly loam
- Rockoway stony loam

C

- Recent alluvium
- Stratified drift
- Till
- Terminal moraine
- Early glacial drift
- Bedrock

A

HACKETTSTOWN

PETTSBOROUGH

BEATYESTOWN

100

miles from the crime scene. This meant that the rocks had been carried to the scene. Further investigation in the nearby area where these rocks outcrop produced a suspect who drove a pickup truck and carried similar rocks to add weight in the back of the truck.

Topographic maps may be of use in some cases. These maps show the elevation of the land above some datum, usually sea level. Through an informer, agents of an Alcohol Beverage Commission had learned that an illegal still existed between two towns, near a railroad, and it had a well in which the water level was twenty feet below the surface of the earth. The last point may seem to be strange information developed in an investigation but would be common knowledge for a well driller. The exact location of the still was not known. Examination of the topographic map revealed that the area was one of swamps and ridges. The ridges were of sand and gravel and at only one place was there an elevation of twenty feet or more above the level of the nearby swamp. Under such conditions it could be assumed that the water level in the ground, and thus in the well, would not be much higher than the elevation of the water table in the swamp. That one possible location was occupied by a church. Further investigation revealed the still in the basement of the church and led to a successful prosecution and destruction of the still.

Collection of Soil Samples

Because of the layering effect in natural soils, samples should be collected by horizon. In most forensic situations, however, comparisons need to be made only between the surface layer and sample in question—therefore, in such cases, only the top layers of the soil need to be collected. Soil samples should be placed in an ice cream carton, plastic vials, or sampling frame (Fig. 6-4). If samples are wet or moist they should be air dried before placing them in a vial or other similar container. Otherwise biological activity will continue, which will cause a breakdown of certain organic components and the formation of new organic-related compounds. Samples which are collected for

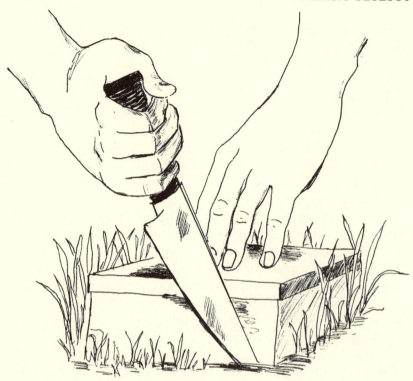

Figure 6-4   Collecting a soil sample in a sampling frame. This method insures a minimum of disturbance of the sample.

conductivity measurements or those containing volatile substances should normally be sealed and refrigerated until
analyzed. The amount of sample required for analysis depends
upon the type of study to be made. Most analyses require approximately one cupful of soil. However, for mechanical
analysis of the particle sizes of soil a larger sample may be
necessary. If there is considerable gravel or other coarse material present the size of the sample should be increased accordingly. However, if large sample sizes are not available the sample
collector should keep in mind that even a few grains of soil are
better than none. The late Professor W. L. Kubiëna stated that
in the plant museums of Europe pedologists had been able to

locate the general area from which plants were collected by examining a few grains of soil clinging to the roots.

Some properties of a soil become altered upon drying but others do not. The main properties of a soil which may be subject to change upon drying are:

1. If salts are present in the sample the salts will be concentrated and may crystallize on the surface of the sample.

2. Some minerals may oxidize or be subject to other alteration and in so doing, may change color. This is especially true of black sulfur-bearing muds from swamps or marshes.

3. Nitrate content of a dried sample tends to increase.

4. Population and activities of microbes will be greatly altered.

5. A soil sample will tend to change to a lighter color upon drying.

In the case of samples collected from certain wet areas such as marshes or bogs it may be desirable to seal them in plastic or glass containers and refrigerate them. In this way there will be unimportant changes through microbial activity or oxidation.

Water samples should be collected in a plastic or glass container sealed and refrigerated. The low temperature will retard biological growth and prevent important changes.

If pollen studies are to be conducted on geologic or soil samples, care must be exercised to prevent pollen contamination. Since there is pollen in the air throughout the year, it is necessary to seal specimens and samples in plastic wrapping so that contamination can be kept to a minimum.

When conditions necessitate an analysis of trace metals, there is always the question of metal contribution to the sample from digging implements, metal containers and sieves themselves. Under such situations it is preferable to use stainless steel implements, storage boxes, and sieves.

In most cases the scientist works with the material submitted by the investigator. In others, situations commonly after examination of the originally submitted material, it may be desirable to collect new or additional material. This is normally done with the help and cooperation of the investigator. The scientist should be careful to restrict himself to questions and information within his professional expertise and not interfere with the professional perogatives, duties, and responsibilities of the investigator. Where the scientist collects material for study with the results to be presented to parties other than the original investigator, he must work in a manner that is appropriate to his professional expertise and observe the methods and procedures that are both legal and appropriate to forensic science. Specifically, the samples must be collected by legal means and the results must be presented as scientific information without consideration of whether the information is favorable or unfavorable to any individual or group.

When the scientist sees that important information might be obtained from additional samples or information, he may arrange to obtain these samples or information. For example, in a case of forceable rape in an area of glacial outwash, the suspect was found to have a large accumulation of sand within his trouser cuffs. The victim had given the investigator the location of the scene of the crime and the investigator had collected soil samples from the scene. When the samples of sand from the suspect's cuffs were studied in connection with samples from the scene they were found to compare. This comparison was made on the basis of ten unusual rock types existing as particles in both samples and in the same percentage of the whole sample. In addition, there were no rock types found in only one of the two samples that did not exist in the other. One of the unusual rock types was fresh anthracite coal. It was known from geologic experience that anthracite coal did not exist naturally in the area and also did not exist north of the area and thus could not be a natural particle in glacial outwash from this place. Despite this, the coal was common in the samples, making up over 5 percent of the particles. Examination of the scene in the company of the investigator revealed that anthracite coal particles were indeed common in the soil at the scene. At this point the investigator established that the scene had been the site of a coal pile for a laundry sixty years earlier. The coal in the soil was apparently the remains of the former pile of coal. This additional information further increased the already high probability that the soil in the suspect's trouser cuffs had been picked up at the scene of the crime.

It is important that one be familiar with the legal and general professional rules involved in this type of study. He should seek competent legal advice before collecting any samples for these purposes with respect to whether the samples are obtained incident to an arrest or whether permission or a warrant is necessary. Most important, he should obtain professional advice with regard to his responsibility for maintaining control over the chain of evidence. That is, the forensic geologist must establish or work within established procedures for the protection of samples and data from contamination, theft, substitution, or alteration while in his custody. In addition, it is important that a written record be kept of the transfer of any material to the scientist's custody and transfer from the scientist's custody to another person.

References

Cline, M. G. 1944. Principles of soil sampling. *Soil Sci.,* 58:275–288.

Eardley, A. J. 1962. *Structural geology of North America.* 2nd ed. New York: Harper and Row.

Kirk, P. L. 1935. *Crime investigation.* New York: Interscience Publishers.

U.S. Department of Agriculture. 1972. *Soil survey laboratory methods and procedures for collecting samples.* Soil Survey Investigations Report, No. 2. Washington, D.C.: U.S. Govt. Prtg. Office.

SOURCES OF GEOLOGIC MAPS AND INFORMATION

ALABAMA
    Geological Survey of Alabama
    P.O. Drawer 0
    University, Alabama 35486

ALASKA
    Division of Geological Survey
    Box 5-300
    College, Alaska 99701

ARIZONA
    Arizona Bureau of Mines
    University of Arizona
    Tucson, Arizona 85721

ARKANSAS
    Arkansas Geological Commission
    State Capitol
    Little Rock, Arkansas 72201

CALIFORNIA
    Department of Conservation
    Division of Mines & Geology
    1416 Ninth Street, Room 1341
    Sacramento, California 95814 .

COLORADO
    Colorado Geological Survey
    1845 Sherman Street, Room 254
    Denver, Colorado 80203

CONNECTICUT
Connecticut Geological and
Natural History Survey
Wesleyan Station
Middletown, Connecticut 06457
DELAWARE
Delaware Geological Survey
University of Delaware
Newark, Delaware 19711
FLORIDA
Bureau of Geology
P.O. Box 631
Tallahassee, Florida 32303
GEORGIA
Department of Mines, Mining &
Geology
19 Hunter St., S.W.
Atlanta, Georgia 30334
HAWAII
Division of Water & Land De-
velopment
Dept. of Land & Natural Resources
P.O. Box 373
Honolulu, Hawaii 96809
IDAHO
Idaho Bureau of Mines and Geol-
ogy
Moscow, Idaho 83843
ILLINOIS
Illinois State Geological Survey
121 Natural Resources Building
Urbana, Illinois 61801
INDIANA
Department of Natural Resources
Geological Survey
611 N. Walnut Grove
Bloomington, Indiana 47401
IOWA
Iowa Geological Survey
16 West Jefferson Street
Iowa City, Iowa 52240
KANSAS
State Geological Survey of Kansas
University of Kansas
Lawrence, Kansas 66044

KENTUCKY
Kentucky Geological Survey
University of Kentucky
307 Mineral Industries Building
Lexington, Kentucky 40506
LOUISIANA
Louisiana Geological Survey
Box G
University Station
Baton Rouge, Louisiana 70803
MAINE
Division of Science
Technology and Mineral Re-
sources
Marden Building, State Street
Augusta, Maine 04330
MARYLAND
Maryland Geological Survey
214 Latrobe Hall
Johns Hopkins University
Baltimore, Maryland 21218
MICHIGAN
Geological Survey Division
Michigan Department of Natural
Resources
Steven T. Mason Building
Lansing, Michigan 48926
MINNESOTA
Minnesota Geological Survey
220 Pillsbury Hall
University of Minnesota
Minneapolis, Minnesota 55455
MISSISSIPPI
Mississippi Geological Survey
2525 North West
P.O. Box 4915
Jackson, Mississippi 39216
MISSOURI
Missouri Geological Survey &
Water Resources
P.O. Box 250
Rolla, Missouri 65401

MONTANA
  Montana Bureau of Mines & Geology
  Main Hall
  Montana Tech
  Butte, Montana 59701
NEVADA
  Nevada Bureau of Mines
  University of Nevada
  Reno, Nevada 89507
NEBRASKA
  Conservation and Survey Division
  113 Nebraska Hall
  University of Nebraska
  Lincoln, Nebraska 68508
NEW HAMPSHIRE
  Dept. of Resources & Economic Development
  James Hall, Univ. of New Hampshire
  Durham, New Hampshire 03824
NEW JERSEY
  Bureau of Geology & Topography
  Room 709, Labor & Industry Bldg.
  John Fitch Plaza, John Fitch Way
  Trenton, New Jersey 08625
NEW MEXICO
  New Mexico State Bureau of Mines & Mineral Resources
  Socorro, New Mexico 87801
NEW YORK
  Geological Survey
  New York State Museum & Science Service
  State Education Department
  Albany, New York 12224
NORTH CAROLINA
  Division of Mineral Resources
  Department of Conservation & Development
  212 Administration Building,
  P.O. Box 27687
NORTH DAKOTA
  North Dakota Geological Survey
  University Station
  Grand Forks, North Dakota 58201

OHIO
  Division of Geological Survey
  1207 Grandview Avenue
  Columbus, Ohio 43212
OKLAHOMA
  Oklahoma Geological Survey
  830 Van Vleet Oval, Room 163
  Norman, Oklahoma 73069
OREGON
  State of Oregon Department of Geology & Mineral Industries
  1069 State Office Building
  Portland, Oregon 97201
PENNSYLVANIA
  Bureau of Topographic & Geologic Survey
  Main Capitol Annex
  Harrisburg, Pennsylvania 17120
PUERTO RICO
  Mineralogy & Geology Section
  Economic Development Administration of Puerto Rico
  Industrial Laboratory
  P.O. Box 38
  Roosevelt, Puerto Rico 00936
SOUTH CAROLINA
  Division of Geology
  South Carolina State Development Board
  Box 927
  Columbia, South Carolina 29202
SOUTH DAKOTA
  South Dakota Geological Survey
  Science Center University
  Vermillion, South Dakota 57069
TENNESSEE
  Department of Conservation
  Division of Geology
  G-5 State Office Bldg.
  Nashville, Tennessee 37219
TEXAS
  Bureau of Economic Geology
  University of Texas at Austin
  University Station, Box X
  Austin, Texas 78712

UTAH
  Geological & Mineralogical Survey
  103 Utah Geological Survey Bldg.
  University of Utah
  Salt Lake City, Utah 84112
VERMONT
  Vermont Geological Survey
  Perkins Hall
  University of Vermont
  Burlington, Vermont 05401
VIRGINIA
  Virginia Division of Mineral Re-
    sources
  P.O. Box 3667
  Charlottesville, Virginia 22903
WASHINGTON
  Washington Division of Mines &
    Geology
  Department of Natural Resources
  P.O. Box 168
  Olympia, Washington 98501

WEST VIRGINIA
  West Virginia Geological &
    Economic Survey
  Mineral Industries Building
  P.O. Box 879
  Morgantown, W. Virginia 26505
WISCONSIN
  Geological and Natural History
    Survey
  University of Wisconsin
  1815 University Avenue
  Madison, Wisconsin 53706
WYOMING
  The Geological Survey of Wyom-
    ing
  P.O. Box 3008
  University Station
  University of Wyoming
  Laramie, Wyoming 82070

Geologic and topographic maps may be obtained in the United States from the U.S. Geological Survey, 1200 South Eads St., Arlington, Va. 22202, or Federal Center, Denver, Colorado 80225. Detailed soil surveys have been published for many parts of the United States. These reports are available from the U.S. Soil Conservation Service, Washington, D.C.

In other countries government surveys and universities provide a similar service.

7 Comparison Methods for Soils and Related Material

This chapter is concerned with the various ways and means of studying minerals, rocks, soils, and related materials. It is primarily a discussion of how quantitative data may be obtained for subsequent judgments of comparison or lack of comparison. The evidential value of some of these methods is greater than others. However, the selection of methods discussed was made on those that have been used for forensic purposes.

Color of Soils and Sediments

Color is one of the most important identifying characteristics of minerals and soils. Minerals form a mosaic of grays, yellows, browns, reds, blacks, and even greens and brilliant purples. Virtually all possible colors of the visible light spectrum are represented. The forensic geologist can usually detect the characteristic red staining on automobile tires from red shale areas or greenish-yellow-colored staining from soils rich in unweathered glauconite but in other situations color alone may not give much of a clue as to origin of the sample.

With most geologic materials and soils the native minerals contribute directly to the soil color. This is particularly true with stream deposits, wind-blown silts, and other recent formations which have been in place a comparatively short period of time. If sands along a river channel are examined, the color of each sand grain can generally be recognized individually; however, after a deposit has weathered for a long period of time, there is a degree of leaching, accumulation and/or movement of substances within the soil. Soil particles become stained, coated, and impregnated with mineral and organic substances, giving the soil an appearance different from its original one. The mineral grains—especially the larger ones—are generally coated. In most situations the coatings on the soil particles consist of iron, aluminum, organic matter, clay, and other substances. The coloring of the coatings alone can give some indication as to the history of the sample. An analogy would be paint on a board; perhaps the paint would be more traceable than the wood itself. It is the quantity and composition of the coatings which usually give the main coloration to the weathered soil or soil material. The "redness" of a soil is not only dependent upon the amount of iron present, but also its state of oxidation, with the highly oxidized condition tending to be of more reddish color. The iron on the coatings of the particles probably is in the form of hematite, limonite, goethite, lepidocrocite, and other iron-rich mineral forms. Black mineral colors in the soil are generally related to manganese or various iron and manganese combinations. Green colors are generally due to concentrations of specific minerals rather than of the mineral coatings. For example, some copper minerals, chlorite and glauconite are usually green. Deep blue to purple coloration in the soil is generally due to the mineral vivianite, an iron phosphate.

Apart from the mineral colors in the soil are those that result from organic matter. The organic litter on the soil surface is generally black. Humus percolates through the mineral horizons giving various dark colors. In some instances the iron and humic acids combine to form a dark reddish brown to nearly black color.

In order to have some uniformity in descriptions of color of geologic materials and soils certain standards have been established. The color standards most frequently used in the United

States are those of the Munsell Color Co.* The color standards are established on three factors: hue, value, and chroma. *Hue* is the dominant spectral color, *value* is the lightness color and *chroma* is the relative purity of the spectral color. Soil and rock colors are generally recorded as, for example, 7.5YR5/2 (brown). The 7.5YR refers to the hue, 5 the value and 2 the chroma.

The above standardization of colors offers some degree of uniformity, but the moisture content will also affect the color of the soil, as will light intensity. If a soil is air dry it may be recorded as yellow, but if moist the recording may be yellowish brown. Moisture added to a dry soil will usually result in a more brilliant appearance. It is therefore not only important to record the color of the soil, but also record an estimate of the "wetness factor" at the time of the recording. In general, colors should be recorded under field conditions as, for example, 7.5YR5/2m (moist) and 7.5YR5/2d (dry).

Soil, being a mixture of materials of various sizes and compositions, contains individual minerals of different colors. If soil is fractionated into various sizes—coarse sand, medium sand, fine sand, silt, and clay, there is a tendency for the finer-sized particles to exhibit more red or reddish brown colors as opposed to grays and yellows in the coarser fractions. In considering coarser sand particles, the matrix will commonly have a speckled appearance with the quartz and feldspar particles being gray or yellowish, but the heavy minerals such as ilmenite and magnetite will generally be black. Sand particles from soils of recent origin, such as recent glacial or stream deposits, usually retain their original mineral appearance and one can usually detect a mosaic of colors. But sand fractions from the old landscapes commonly have coatings of clay and the sand grains may be iron-stained which result in a more uniform color of the entire matrix. Soil grains when veneered with organic matter give the particles a dark gray appearance. It is important first to record the color of the untreated soil sample and then treat it with hydrogen peroxide (to oxidize the organic matter) so that the true color and appearance of the sand grains can be studied.

* 10 East Franklin St., Baltimore, Md.

The fine material, particularly that of clay size (<0.002 mm), is primarily a weathered product from what was originally coarser grained particles. The clay usually has an appreciable quantity of iron present which imparts a reddish color to the sample. If one were to make comparisons between comparable size-groups of soil particles from different sites the coarser particles may show considerable diversity, but the clays may be nearly identical—not only in color, but also in mineral composition.

In studying soil samples for forensic purposes the sample is normally dried at approximately 100° C. and viewed with natural light preferably coming from a northerly direction. A north-facing window is a good location for such observations. Such studies should be made on samples that have the same general size distribution of particles. Color of samples prepared from the individual sieved-out particle size ranges gives important additional data. Two or more samples, collected for study, can be compared directly by the observer. It is then possible to use a color chart with the samples to determine the Munsell color numbers for precise description of the color.

Density Distribution of Particles

The density of a mineral, rock, or other solid particle, that is, the weight of the particle per unit volume, is usually expressed as grams per cubic centimeter. The density will be different for each particle depending on the minerals present and the chemical composition of the particle. It will also depend on how much pore space exists between the mineral grains and whether bubbles exist within the minerals (fluid inclusions). The density of individual common mineral particles varies over a wide range from almost 20 grams per cubic centimeter for gold to carnallite which has a density of only 1.7 grams per cubic centimeter. Some particles found in soils, particularly those of an organic nature, have a density less than that of water. Most organic particles are assumed to have a density approximating 0.9 that of water. The density of a material when compared with the density of water at 4° C. (1.00) is called the *specific gravity* (Sp. G.) and is usually expressed as the number of times the material is denser than that of water. For example, pure quartz has a specific gravity of 2.65. Because the density of individual particles varies, the distribution of densities of the various particles in a soil sample can be used for determining whether one sample of soil is similar to another. The *density gradient column* technique is perhaps the most common method used for soil comparison for forensic purposes. The method has been described by a number of authors (Kirk, 1943; Nickolls, 1962; and others).

When two dried samples of soil are to be compared they are first carefully pulverized with a rubber tool and then placed on a nest of sieves to separate the sample into different size fractions. Comparison should be made on only those sizes in the control sample that exist in the associated or questioned sample. The smaller of the two samples, usually the associated or questioned sample, is weighed and an equal amount from the control sample is also weighed. If the sample weighs more than 75 mg, a tube larger than 10 mm inside diameter would be necessary to carry out the study. It is especially important that the two samples be of the same weight because it is the concentration of densities that is to be studied. The columns are glass tubes usually twelve to eighteen inches in length that have been sealed at the bottom. The tubes are placed in a rack and filled with liquids of different densities. The heaviest liquid is first placed in the tube followed by liquids of decreasing densities, usually ten in all. The columns are then allowed to stand in an upright position until the liquids have had a chance to mix by diffusion and a column of liquid that decreases uniformly upward in density is produced. This usually takes place in twenty-four to forty-eight hours. It is extremely important that the two columns be produced in exactly the same way, that is, the same amount of each liquid added in exactly the same way. This is necessary because the two columns are to be compared. It is also important that the two be at the same temperature because the liquids change their density with temperature.

The liquids used in the density column may vary from one laboratory to another. However, the most commonly used are bromoform (density 2.89) and bromobenzene (density 1.499).

The two liquids are mixed in fixed amounts such as five volumes of bromobenzene to one volume of bromoform. Ten liquids of different densities from pure bromoform to pure bromo- benzene are produced. It is these mixed standard liquids that are placed layer by layer in the columns.

When the two columns have "equilibrated" and produced a uniform density gradient in the liquid, the two samples of equal weight are placed, one in each column. Within a few hours the individual particles of the soils settle to a level in the column where the liquid has the same density as that of the individual particle. Thus the particles will be distributed in the column according to the different densities represented in the sample (Fig. 7-1). Size of particle (except possibly some of the ultrafine clay) in itself will have no influence on the level a particle seeks; only the density of the particle is important. Some of the smaller particles may take longer to come to a position of rest. If the sample has a large proportion of very fine particles it may take up to two days to settle without further particle movement.

The distribution of particles in the two tubes is examined and commonly photographed. The pictures, which may be pre- sented as evidence, should be taken against a uniform white background lighted with a fluorescent or other cool light. Glass or other transparent particles may require lighting from above or below. A cool light is necessary because heat will cause convection currents to disrupt the density column liquids. The two samples are said to compare when the distribution of de- nsities of particles appears the same in the two columns. A difference of 0.01 grams/cm^3 in any one segment of the density column can easily be detected. A comparison of the two samples, however, involves some professional judgment.

The value of the method lies in the ease with which com- parisons can be made on a routine basis. In addition, the method can be standardized, that is, used in the same way in different laboratories by different people, and the columns can be pre- pared by any skilled technician. Human errors in preparing the columns can be kept to a minimum. Unfortunately, this method has commonly been used as the sole method of comparison in many cases and presented as the only scientific evidence for

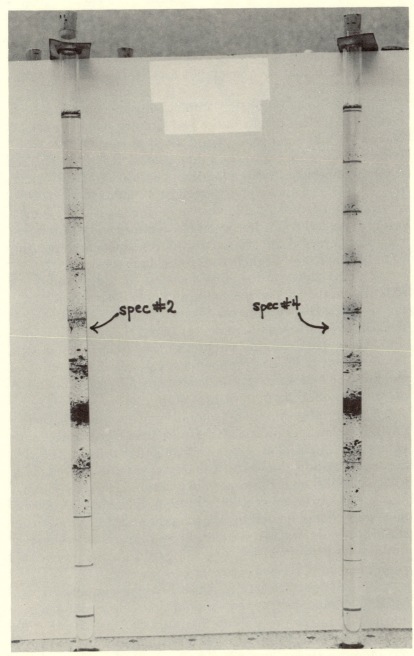

Figure 7-1 Density column for the determination of the density distribution of particles. *Courtesy of New Jersey State Police.*

comparison of soils. Because of this, it is well to examine the geologic problems as opposed to the problems involved in preparation of the columns. Several of these problems are:

1. The breaking of the samples with the rubber tool may produce different results in the two samples. This is especially true if one has been pressed and dried as is often true with a sample from a shoe and the other is loose material. This can result in mineral particles adhering to each other. If, for example, a particle of mica with a density of 3.0 sticks to a particle of quartz with a density of 2.65, the composite particle will come to rest in the column at a density level somewhere between the two values, whereas if the two particles remained separate they would come to rest at their own individual density levels.

2. The density for the heaviest liquid, bromoform ($CHBr_3$), at the base of the column is 2.89. This means that all the so-called "heavy minerals," which can be so diagnostic in forensic soil studies, and are denser than 2.89 fall to the bottom and accumulate. Another common heavy liquid used is tetrabromoethane ($C_2H_2Br_4$) with a density of 2.97. Even using this fluid for the bottom layer will cause many different minerals to accumulate at the bottom of the column.

3. The most common mineral in natural soils is quartz. Quartz very commonly makes up more than 80 percent of individual soil samples. Pure quartz has a fixed density of 2.65. The density of an individual particle of quartz or most other minerals will change if fluid inclusions, solid inclusions, and particle coatings such as iron minerals, are present. Thus the particles of most soils are dominated by one mineral with the same density. Differences observed in the density column result from small variations, such as inclusions or coatings, that might or might not be significant, if studied separately.

4. If the particles are rocks and have some porosity, it is possible for air to be trapped within the particle, making it more buoyant. How the two soils are handled and treated can cause differences in density in such particles that would otherwise be considered geologically similar.

5. The measurement of any property without actually de-

termining what causes the differences can lead to error. In soil samples, quartz and some of the common feldspars have about the same density and will appear at the same level in the column.

In the light of these problems it can be concluded that the density distribution column method, however carefully done by the scientist, has severe limitations. This is true despite empirical studies which have shown that samples from different places commonly give different distributions and samples from the same place commonly show distributions that are very much alike. If the density distributions are very dissimilar then there is probably little likelihood that they compare. If the differences are relatively small then they may or may not compare. If there are no observable differences, then it is likely that they compare insofar as the measured property is concerned. In the latter cases the prudent scientist would want to confirm the judgment with other methods. This is consistent with the statement of Frenkel (1968) who said, "Published results on the pattern of a soil in a density gradient tube (Goin and Kirk, 1947; Peters, 1962) are sufficient to indicate, but are not sufficient to demonstrate, that this may be a significant forensic property."

Size Distribution of Soils and Sediments

The forensic geologist is often faced with the problem of determining the distribution of sizes of particles in a sample. The purpose may be (1) to produce samples for comparison studies that are similar, in which case, the control sample may contain some large or smaller particles that are not present in the questioned or associated sample and they must be removed; (2) the samples may be broken down into subsamples in which all the particles are in the same size range for mineral or color studies; (3) a determination of the distribution of sizes of particles may be produced as a method of comparison. A diagram showing the distribution of grain sizes can be used as a comparison method and in some cases may be of evidential value. For example, when abrasive particles have been introduced into machinery for the purpose of sabotage the size distribution of the particles may be diagnostic of the material assuming that changes in particle size have not taken place in the machinery.

The basic methods used for separation of sizes are (1) passing the sample through a nest of wire sieves with the size of the openings decreasing from top to bottom, or (2) determining the rate of settling of the grains in a fluid which is a measure of the size of the particles. In the case of sieving and some of the settling methods, the weight of material in each particle size range is determined and plotted on diagrams.

Before making mechanical analysis to determine the size distribution of particles, it is necessary to disperse the soil. Individual soil particles tend to stick together in the form of aggregates. Cementing agents of the aggregates must be removed, otherwise a cluster of silt and clay particles would have the physical dimensions of sand or gravel. Cementing agents consist of organic matter, accumulated carbonates, iron oxide coatings, and in some situations there simply is a mutual attraction of particles by physicochemical forces.

If carbonates have cemented the particles together it is desirable to pretreat the sample with dilute hydrochloric acid to remove the carbonates. The sample is then treated with hydrogen peroxide to remove the organic cementing agents. Naturally, all samples must be treated in the same way and it must be determined before treatment that important information will not be lost.

It is almost always desirable to determine size distribution of soil by sieving in a liquid, usually water. Dry sieving of the entire sample is generally unsatisfactory because the small particles tend to cluster together and clay tends to adhere to larger particles. Sometimes a dispersing agent is added to the water.

There are a number of methods that can then be used for determining the size distribution of the finer particles in a dispersed suspension. The *hydrometer method* is a rapid method for determining the percentage of sand, silt, and clay in a sample and it is based on the principle of a decreasing density of the suspension as the solid particles settle out. This method, while rapid and accurate, is unsatisfactory if one wants to make subsequent examination of the various size ranges because there is actually no physical separation of the various-sized particles.

One of the most accurate and satisfactory procedures for fractionating soil samples is by the *pipette method*. This consists of pretreating the sample as is done in the hydrometer method, dispersing the soil in water and calculating the time required for various-sized particles to settle out from the suspension. The principle is based on the fact that the rate of settling depends upon the size of the mineral matter with larger particles settling at a more rapid rate. The procedure is based on *Stokes' Law:* $V = {}^2/_9\ gr^2\ (d - d')/n$. $V =$ velocity of fall in cm/sec, g is the acceleration due to gravity, r is the radius of the particle in cm, d is the density of the particle in gm/cc, d' is the density of the fluid in gm/cc and n is the viscosity of the fluid in poises. Although this method is generally considered the most satisfactory in regard to accuracy it is not infallible. Several assumptions are made —namely, that all particles have the same shape and that all the soil particles have the same density, neither of which is the case. Nevertheless, the pipette method is generally considered to be the best available method.

Other methods of making separations of soil particles are: *elutriation, decantation, centrifugation* and the *plummet* method (Kilmer and Alexander, 1949).

In making a mineral analysis of a sample one fact becomes apparent, that is, the sample contains different groups of minerals within various size ranges. Sands are made up of a set of minerals which are usually completely different from those within the clay size range. Therefore, in comparative analysis it is important to make comparisons within the same size ranges. It can be quite deceptive to compare the minerals found in one size range in one sample with a different size range in another sample.

Stereo Binocular Microscope

The stereo binocular microscope can be a most useful tool to the forensic geologist (Fig. 7-2). After an analysis of color has been made, the information that can be obtained by examination

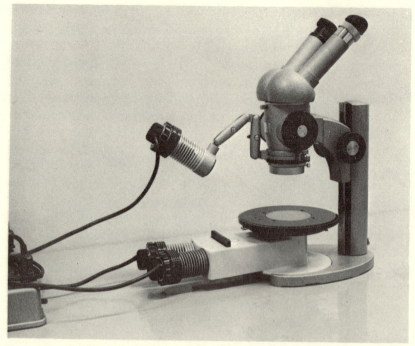

Figure 7-2   Stereo binocular microscope. This particular instrument can also be used for viewing in transmitted polarized light.

of soil samples with this instrument makes it the logical second step in any comparison study.

Light microscopes are generally of two types, *transmitted* light and *reflected* light. In transmitted light microscopes the light source is placed beneath the specimen, which must be transparent. Biological microscopes that are used in studying tissue are of this type. Reflected light microscopes have a light source above the object and the surface features of the particle are viewed. Such a microscope is really a stationary, higher-power magnifying glass. Most of these microscopes have two sets of lenses and thus the object is viewed in three dimensions, that is in stereo. The magnification of a microscope is determined by multiplying the magnification of the ocular lens, commonly 10×, by the magnification of the objective lens which differs from microscope to microscope but seldom exceeds 10×. This gives a maximum magnification of approximately 100×. The objectives may be individual lenses of fixed magnification, or in some microscopes a zoom objective is used. Such lenses can change magnification continuously from less than 1× to about 4×. Most viewing with stereo binocular microscopes is done at magnification between 10× and 40×. Some of these microscopes are seated on a base that contains a second light source so that objects can be viewed in both transmitted and reflected light. When the transmitted light is polarized (see section on the petrographic microscope) the microscope may be used for both stereo reflected light viewing and low-power transmitted polarizing light studies.

Objects as small as approximately 10 microns in diameter are viewed with the stereo binocular microscope. The upper limit is determined by how large a sample can fit under the instrument so that the surface of pebbles and cobbles can easily be viewed. The sample is normally placed on a tray having a dull black finish for ease of viewing light-colored minerals or white finish for viewing dark-colored minerals. Various inserts are available for these microscopes that permit measurement of the size of objects or provide grids that aid in the counting of the various particles. The sample tray may have an etched grid that serves a similar purpose. Trays are available with various gummed surfaces that hold the grains in place for ease of counting.

In examining a soil sample or similar material the scientist will commonly first examine the whole sample as it is received and observe the types of grains and particles (Fig. 7-3). Recording a general impression of the material is normally done at this time. It is not uncommon to observe in soil samples nonmineral materials such as fibers, metals, paint, glass, plastics, etc. These objects can have important evidential value. In some situations they can be the most important parts of the sample. Materials such as hair, fibers, paint, and plastic are removed for further examination by specialists. Plant particles can be of great value. The total amount of plant material is in general relatively useless for forensic purposes. However, the identification of the individual grasses, seeds, leaves, etc., can be most useful.

Following a bank holdup, the getaway vehicle was aban-

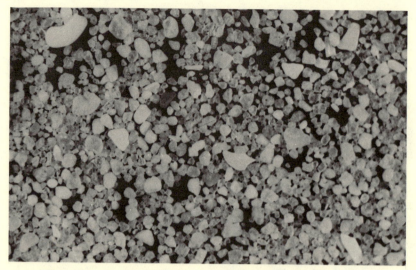

Figure 7-3   Beach sand as seen under a binocular microscope.

doned and the suspects picked up another car that had been parked in a rural wooded area adjacent to a field. They were apprehended in the second vehicle but refused to reveal the location of the original getaway car. Examination was made of soil removed from the frame and fenders of the second car. There was a great deal of soil on this car, indicating that it had been driven off the pavement through moist soil. During the binocular microscopic examination the soil was found to contain hair from both brown and black cows and a palomino horse. From the seeds, leaves, and other particles of vegetation it was possible to reconstruct the types of plants that grew in the area where the soil was picked up by the car. Examination of the mineral material showed that the soil was formed by the weathering of limestone and the area must be underlain by limestone rock. It was possible to recognize the limestone as coming from a particular type of rock that was found in the area and underlay several square miles. Armed with this information, investigators drove the back roads of the area underlain by the particular limestone, looking for a field with the particular vegetation and having the right animals. Such a field was found and the missing car was discovered in the woods on the edge of the field. The discovery of the getaway car proved to have considerable value when combined with evidence from the suspect car in reconstructing the crime and leading to the conviction of the suspects.

In a suburb of Sydney, Australia, in 1960, the eight-year-old son of a recent lottery winner was kidnapped and murdered. Six weeks after the kidnapping the victim's body was found by boys playing in a wooded area. Examination of the victim's clothing with the binocular microscope revealed, among other bits of evidence, some pink chips composed of grains of sand in a matrix that reacted with hydrochloric acid, the mineral calcite. These chips were recognized as small pieces of a mortar used in house construction in the area, especially in one-family houses on high foundations. In addition, among the plant material that was removed for study by botanists abundant parts of two cypresses were found, *Chamaecyparis pisifera*, variety *squjarrosa* and *Cypressus glabra*. The first is fairly common as an ornamental plant. The second is rather rare. Examination of samples from the scene where the body was found failed to uncover evidence of either plant or particles of the mortar. Thus it was reasoned that the victim had first been taken to a house with pink mortar that had both varieties of cypress trees. Investigators, carrying examples of branches from the two cypresses and knowledge of the pink mortar, scoured the area for weeks. Several houses had the pink mortar, but lacked the cypresses. Finally, a house with all three was found. The occupants had recently moved to that house but investigation revealed that the former occupants had moved out on the day of the murder. Further investigation showed that the former occupant was a prime suspect. He was identified and convicted.

In the comparison of soils, particles such as paint, glass, plastics, and metals can be extremely useful and can be treated as diagnostic elements in the soil. Their value, as with any other particle, lies in how common and widely distributed they are. Examination of objects left at the scene of a crime can contain many mineral particles. There are many examples in which the occupation of the owner of the object has been deduced from analyses of such particles. A classic case involved the deduction that the suspect was a left-handed cutter of Douglas fir wood, from the chips of this wood in the right-hand pocket of trousers. Presence of the various industrial minerals such as asbestos, gypsum as used in wall board, talc, salt, limestone, etc., can prove useful. For example, the gloves of a dairy farmer contained traces of yellow salt sold commercially as salt lick blocks for cattle. Preliminary examination of the whole sample with the binocular microscope is normally very difficult. The mixture of particles of all sizes commonly obscures the grains and makes identification difficult. Presence of organic material contributes to this problem. The sample must be cleaned for study of minerals and rock. Sieving of the samples removes the larger particles and most of the larger organic fragments. If the sample is carefully washed in water, the lighter organic particles will generally float and can be removed and saved for study. Treatment with hydrogen peroxide will remove the fine organic matter and clean the sample. The use of ultrasonic cleaners is dangerous in many cases. Many times the scientist has taken a sample that contained chips of red shale before ultrasonic cleaning and found that his sample contained thousands of silt-size quartz grains and clay minerals after cleaning and that the shale chips had been eliminated. If the rocks and minerals are of a kind that would not be disaggregated by ultrasonic cleaning then the method can be most useful.

With a clean sample the experienced scientist can identify the rocks and minerals at sight or by using simple tests such as hydrochloric acid for carbonate minerals, a magnet for magnetite, diagnostic stains for dolomite, feldspar, etc. In addition, it is possible to observe the texture and coatings on the surface of the grains. Properties of grains such as shape, rounding, weathering, inclusions, color, polish, etc., can be observed and recorded.

Counting of different kinds of grains is especially important. When we record our information in numbers it is normally more useful than qualitative impressions. As discussed in Chapter 2, it is unrealistic to expect that any two samples will have exactly the same characteristics. However, the number or percentage of different types of grains is an extremely important tool in determining comparison or lack of comparison. In counting grains of different types it is important that the sample counted be representative of the whole sample, that the identification be consistent and accurate, and that the same grain not be counted twice because the sample moved. The last named problem can usually be avoided by placing the sample on a gummed surface or by removing the grains as they are counted and placing each grain, as it is removed, in a container or gummed individual tray. Most important is the judgment and caution used by the scientist, whatever method is used.

Examination of rocks is commonly made with the stereo binocular microscope. Much can be learned in this way. However, further study of the rock in "thin section" may be required (see *Petrographic Microscope*). In one interesting case a shipment of gold bars was sent to England by plane. When the wooden boxes were opened on arrival they were found to contain a collection of stream-worn pebbles rather than gold. This was rather upsetting to the owner, the insurance company, and the airline. Examination of the pebbles showed that they were not English and were derived from rocks found in the Alps and thus common in certain rivers that flow from the Alps to the sea. The plane had stopped in Milan, Italy, and the transfer had taken place there, prior to arrival in England.

The Petrographic (Polarizing) Microscope

A polarizing microscope differs in detail from an ordinary compound microscope (Fig. 7-4). However, its primary function is the same: to produce an enlarged image of an object placed on the stage. The magnification is produced by a combination of two sets of lenses, the objective and the ocular. The function of the objective lens, at the lower end of the microscope tube, is to produce an image that is sharp and clear. The ocular lens merely enlarges this image. For mineralogical work three objectives, low-, medium-, and high-powered are normally used. The magnification produced by objectives is usually $2\times$ (low), $10\times$ (medium), and $50\times$ (high). Oculars have different magnifications, usually $5\times$, $7\times$, $10\times$. The total magnification of the image

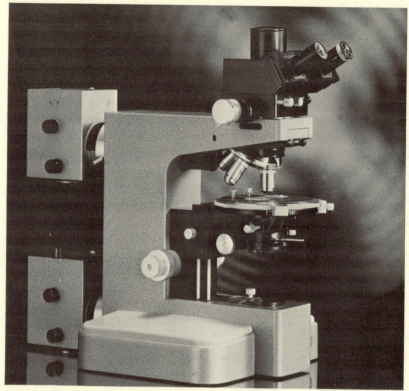

Figure 7-4 Binocular petrographic microscope. *Courtesy of E. Leitz & Co.*

is determined by multiplying the magnification of the objective by that of the ocular as: 50× *times* 10× = 500×.

Oculars normally contain a cross hair which is useful for locating grains under high power when changing objectives. A condensing lens system is normally provided under the stage for use with high magnification and for assisting the viewing of the various optical effects produced by minerals. Petrographic microscopes have a rotating stage and a polarizing filter under the stage that transmits light vibrating in a N-S direction (front-back). Above the stage a second, removable polarizing filter is placed in the tube of the microscope. It transmits light in an E-W (left-right) direction. When the upper filter is inserted, light is blocked out from passing through the microscope. In this case the filters, which are called polars, are said to be *crossed*. Only when an anisotropic material, that is a mineral that is not isotropic (meaning it forms in the isometric crystal system or is amorphous), is placed on the microscope stage under crossed polars can it be seen. The effect of the anisotropic mineral is to rotate the N-S vibrating light from the lower polarizing filter, thus permitting some of it to pass the upper E-W polarizing filter. When the stage is rotated there will be four positions when the vibration directions in an anisotropic crystal will line up with the N-S and E-W direction. At these positions the crystal is said to be at *extinction* and will appear black, thus not be seen.

In identifying mineral grains under the petrographic microscope it is common to use the *immersion method*. Mineral grains are placed on a microscope slide in a liquid of known refractive index. These liquids are available commercially. The range 1.46 to 1.62 with difference of 0.02 between adjacent liquids serve most purposes. When the grain is viewed, a narrow line of light is commonly seen surrounding the grain. If the tube of the microscope is raised slightly, the line of light, called a *Becke line*, will move in the direction of the higher refractive index. If the mineral has a higher refractive index, the Becke line will move into the grain. If the liquid of known refractive index is higher, the Becke line will move away from the grain into the liquid.

By trial and error with different liquids a match is found. At this point the grain will be almost invisible in the liquid. In most cases the refractive index of the grain is found to fall between the refractive indices of two liquids and the value can be estimated by the experienced observer.

Consider a mineral in the isometric crystal system. It will be isotropic, that is having only one refractive index. Thus it will remain dark at all positions under crossed polars. With the upper polarizing filter removed, it will be seen and its refractive index can be determined. Knowing the refractive index and the fact that it is in the isometric crystal system, plus observations on color, cleavage etc., it is possible for the microscopist to identify the mineral.

For minerals that form in the other crystal systems, more information is easily obtainable. Hexagonal and tetragonal minerals have two refractive indices. In addition it is possible to find out whether the mineral is positive or negative. This is determined by using accessories that are inserted into the microscope and depends on which of the two refractive indices is higher. For these minerals identification is made using the two indices of refraction, the optical sign (positive or negative) and the other properties. Several books are available that list the optical properties that facilitate identification. (For example, see McCrone and Delly, 1973).

The petrographic (polarizing) microscope is an important tool in many aspects of forensic work and is the best method for the study of the optical properties of rocks and minerals. Study of individual mineral grains or *thin sections* of rocks and related material is easily accomplished by anyone trained in the use of the instrument (Fig. 7-5). A thin section is a thin slice of rock mounted on a glass slide. The slice is normally 30 microns in thickness and may be prepared from a solid rock or loose material impregnated with plastic. The rock is cut with a diamond saw and the surface polished. This polished surface is cemented to a glass microscope slide with an adhesive of known refractive index such as Epoxy or Canada Balsam. A saw cut is then made parallel to the glass, leaving a wafer of rock cemented on the slide. Grinding of the wafer proceeds until it is thinned to approximately 30 microns. Most rocks are transparent at this

Figure 7-5   Left, thin section of one kind of igneous rock (basalt); *right,* sedimentary rock (sandstone) seen through a petrographic microscope.

thickness and can be viewed in transmitted light. Loose mineral grains of the same general size also commonly mounted in Epoxy or Canada Balsam on a microscope slide are covered with a thin platelet of glass (cover glass) and studied. This is the method used when the *heavy minerals,* that is, those minerals with high specific gravity (such as rutile, garnet, zircon, tourmaline, etc.), are separated from the more common lighter minerals (such as quartz and feldspar) by settling in a heavy liquid such as bromoform, and studied.

In a well-known case where the petrographic microscope played a prominent role, the study led to the conviction of a thief of sheep wool. A suspect who had possession of a number of the fleeces in Wyoming claimed that they had been obtained from sheep in an area distant from the scene of the theft. The crime scene was underlain by isolated outcrops of weathered red shale and sandstone of the Permian Satanka formation. Study of the dust on the wool with the petrographic microscope indicated that the minerals were the same as those found in the area of the red shales and sandstones and were different from those found in the area where the suspect claimed the sheep grazed.

The polarizing microscope is useful for identifying a wide variety of materials other than minerals and glass. Starch grains are one such material as are most of the synthetic crystals such as abrasives, cements, ceramic materials, etc. In an interesting case of murder, the body of the victim was found in a shed that was normally used for storage of garbage. The floor was covered with smashed potatoes and potato skins. A suspect was found whose shoes were covered with starch. Certainly this would be true for anyone walking on the floor of the shed. However, the starch on the suspect's shoes was determined, with the polarizing microscope, to be wheat starch, not potato starch. This was not unreasonable considering that the suspect worked in a bakery whose floor was covered with wheat flour.

Identification of Rocks in Thin Section

Thin section information is often useful in identification and comparison with other rocks. A case in point was the prob-

lem submitted to, and solved by the Pennsylvania Geological
Survey and reported in their periodical *Pennsylvania Geology*.

The Industrial Development Department of the Penn Central Transportation Company submitted two rock samples to the
Survey with the following problem: New automobiles from Detroit were arriving in New Jersey with smashed windows, dents,
and scars resulting from rocks thrown at the passing railroad
cars. The problem was whether, from an examination of the
rocks found in the automobiles, the location of the vandalism
could be identified, so that concentrated policing procedures
could be initiated. Obviously, the whole length of track between
Michigan and New Jersey could not be policed. In addition,
there were two routes that could have been used to transport the
automobiles, one through New York State and one through
Pennsylvania, making any policing job even more difficult.

Along those two railroad routes there is an incredible variety of rock types and many of them can be found at several
different places along the two routes. Thin sections of the rocks
that caused the damage were examined microscopically in the
Pennsylvania Geological Survey laboratory. Both were found to
be a coarse-grained (pegmatitic) gneiss containing feldspar,
quartz, biotite mica, chlorite, and slender crystals, probably of
the mineral apatite. These minerals and the rock texture provided the critical clue that the rock specimens were from a
metamorphic terrain.

The mineralogy of the rock samples permitted the search to
be narrowed to southeastern New York and Pennsylvania.
These areas, known as the Reading Prong in New York and the
Piedmont in Pennsylvania, both contain metamorphic rocks.
The rock type of the samples recovered from the damaged
vehicles occurs along the Penn Central Railroad in Pennsylvania,
but there it usually has less biotite and seldom any apatite. On the
other hand, rocks containing these minerals are common in a
limited area of southeastern New York State. The Survey suggested that the most likely source of the thrown rocks would be
along a stretch of tracks in the vicinity of West Point, north of
New York City. This was confirmed by Penn Central's own
geologists in an independent study of only the northern route.

Penn Central Railroad police concentrated on the West Point area. Several of the culprits were spotted doing the damage and apprehended.

Heavy Minerals

Heavy minerals are those with a specific gravity generally greater than 2.89. They usually represent only a small part of a soil sample but can be very useful for characterizing the material. For this reason, heavy minerals have long been used in geologic studies that attempt to recognize similar rocks and to determine the kinds of rocks that were weathered to produce the particles for sedimentary rocks.

Prior to the separation of the heavy minerals using heavy liquids such as bromoform, the sample is first fractionated into size ranges. Various size ranges can be selected for study but the size range between 0.5 and 0.1 mm is commonly used. The minerals are concentrated by settling in the heavy liquid and are then transferred to a microscope slide covered with a mounting medium of known refractive index such as Lakeside 70 or Canada Balsam. Then they are studied with the polarizing microscope. The individual mineral grains are identified and counted (Fig. 7-6). The results generally are reported as percentage of each mineral of the total. Opaque grains such as magnetite and ilmenite are usually grouped together; however, they may be identified by polishing the surfaces of the opaque grains and studying them under a *reflecting polarizing microscope* of the type used in metallography, where polished surfaces of metals are examined.

There have been many cases in which heavy minerals, combined with other types of observations, have been of important evidential value. In one example where the murder victim's body was found on a New England beach, the suspect stated that the sand in his shoes was picked up by walking on nearby beaches but that he had never walked on the beach where the crime was committed. Studies of the heavy minerals in the sand of the crime scene beach and nearby beaches demonstrated that the minerals were similar to those found on the beach where the

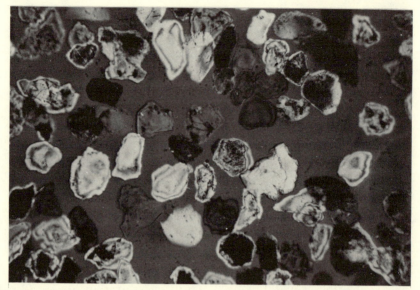

Figure 7-6 Mineral grains mounted on a glass slide and viewed through a petrographic microscope.

body was found and not similar to the sands of the other beaches. The most diagnostic mineral in this case was the rather rare black tourmaline Schorlite, which varied widely in its abundance from location to location.

In a remarkable example of mineral study for forensic purposes, a number of trees replanted on the suspect's property were shown by study of the soil adhering to their roots to be similar to the soil found in holes from which the trees had been removed by theft. In fact, it was possible in this case to actually show, for most of the trees, which tree came from which hole. In the case of one hole no tree could be found that provided a comparison and it could be presumed that this tree was not recovered.

Smale and Trueman (1969) and Smale (1973) have demonstrated the evidential value of heavy mineral studies in the Da Costa murder case. In January of 1968, the body of a man named Koklas was discovered in Australia near the Barkly Highway, apparently a murder victim. A rather complicated set of circumstances led to the arrest in Perth of a suspect named Da Costa who had been thought to be traveling with the murdered man. The suspect admitted having been with Koklas from Melbourne to Mt. Isa, but claimed to have argued with him and left him at Mt. Isa, taking some of his possessions. Among these was a pair of bloodstained shorts, with sand adhering to the bloodstains. Mt. Isa is over 300 miles east of the place where the body was discovered, but it was suspected that the shorts had been removed from the body where it lay, and a study was made of the sand on the shorts with that at the scene of the crime. This was done by examinations of the heavy minerals in the sand. Those on the shorts were consistent with having come in the main from the sand at the scene, with slight contamination. A series of additional samples collected from the area were also examined to determine the degree of variation in the heavy minerals in the area, and the tourmaline grains in the samples were analyzed by using the electron probe micronanalyzer. The variations in the heavy minerals present, and in the tourmaline compositions, showed that the samples closer to the scene compared more closely with the sample from the scene, and it could thus be established that the sand on the shorts was much more likely to have come from the scene of the crime than elsewhere in the area, or from Mt. Isa. The suspect, after a lower-court hearing, admitted that he had been at the scene of the crime.

In glacial sands, silts, and similar material the identification and counting of mineral grains, both heavy and light minerals, have been shown to have very important evidential value. Studies by O. J. Frenkel have shown the great variability and rapid horizontal changes in properties that exist in such sands and silts. These studies provide the basis for a systematic procedure for study of certain light and heavy minerals for forensic purposes in Ontario.

Refractive Index

The index of refraction of a transparent material is the ratio of the velocity of light in a vacuum, normally considered to be 1, to the velocity of light in the material being analyzed. Thus a refractive index of 2.4553 means that light travels 2.4553 times as fast in a vacuum than in the transparent material. The measurement of refractive index, which is the most important method for the comparison of *glass*, may be made using the *Becke line* method discussed for minerals. This method will produce results accurate to ±0.003 when performed by a competent scientist. However, more accurate results can be obtained with less effort using either the *single or double variation method*. In the single variation method the chip of glass is placed in a liquid of known refractive index on the microscope slide. The liquid chosen should be one that changes refractive index with change in temperature. The microscope stage has a heating element and the slide is slowly warmed. As the liquid becomes warmer, its index changes. When the liquid and the glass match, the temperature is observed and recorded. Tables are available which show the refractive index of these liquids at different temperatures. Knowing the temperature, the refractive index of the liquid and the glass can be determined. It is possible to check the refractive index of the liquid at any temperature using glasses of accurately known refractive index.

Refractive index liquids show dispersion, that is, they have a different refractive index in different colored light. Thus the color of the light may be varied until a match is produced and the refractive index of the glass determined. This is possible because glass, like most other solids, shows little dispersion compared to liquids. When the two methods are combined, temperature and color, the method is called double variation. The standard refractive index is that obtained when the orange light (5893 Angstrom units wave length) is used and it is this value, sodium D, that is commonly reported. Using these methods, accuracy better than ±0.001 can be obtained. Variation in the color of the light permits the direct measurement of dispersion, that is, the difference in refractive index that is obtained when blue (4861 Angstrom units) and red light (6563 Angstrom units) are used in the measurement. Indices of refraction and dispersion are the two most commonly used properties in the identification of glass.

One problem with the identification of glass is that quality control and uniformity of production have reduced the range of refractive index found in common glass. For example, prior to 1940 window glass manufactured in England varied from an index of 2.3 to 2.75. Today the range is closer to 2.43 to 2.52. Thus, to be forensically useful, the measurement is made in many laboratories with a *phase contrast microscope*. Phase contrast results when certain additions are made to the microscope that improve observation and the determination of refractive index. When such a microscope is used with a heating microscope stage attached to a Mettler temperature control, it is possible to detect refractive index differences of only 0.00004. This is possible because many refractive index liquids drop in index 0.0004 for each °C. the liquid is heated. The Mettler heating stage can be controlled to 0.1° C. (Fig. 7-7). The temperature at which a refractive index match is found is recorded. Comparison is then made by noting whether the temperatures are similar for two samples. It is important to know the variation in refractive index

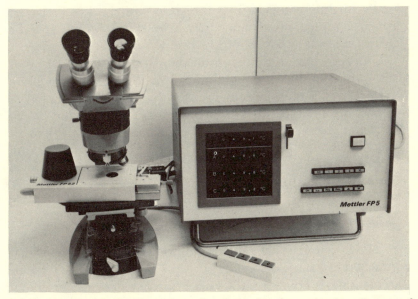

Figure 7-7   Mettler hot stage for refractive index determination. *Courtesy of New Jersey State Police*

within a single piece of glass in determining whether the questioned and control samples compare. For example, a single piece of plate glass can have refractive index differences of 0.0001.

Specific gravity is commonly obtained by comparison of glass fragments in a heavy liquid. The two fragments of glass are placed in a tube with a heavy liquid such as bromoform. This liquid is diluted with a lighter liquid such as ethyl alcohol. The glass fragments will sink if they are denser than the liquid. If they sink, more of the heavier liquid is added until they float freely in the liquid, neither rising nor falling. If both fragments float in this way, they have the same specific gravity. If one very slowly rises or sinks with respect to the other they do not have the same specific gravity but are close enough to be within the variation found in a single large pane of glass, 0.0003 grams per cubic centimeter. It is important that the two liquids be thoroughly mixed and maintained at a constant temperature. In this method the actual specific gravity is not determined. However, this is not important as the two glass samples are actually directly compared. If the shapes of the two pieces of glass are remembered and they are of different specific gravities, then it is possible to recognize which is the denser.

Other properties that are useful in studying comparison of glasses are color in white light and ultraviolet light (see Ch. 8), and thickness. It must be remembered that the thickness of glass is almost never uniform. This is especially true for hand-blown glass. In some cases it is actually possible to mechanically fit chips of glass back together and to match the characteristic marking produced on the broken surface. This results in a very high level of confidence in the comparison.

Cathodoluminescence

The instrument used in this method is a luminoscope which is attached as a stage on a microscope. The specimen—grains or thin section—is bombarded with a beam of electrons generated by the instrument. When the electrons strike the surface of the specimen an optical luminescence is produced which is seen as a display of colors. The color and intensity of the colors depends in large part on very small changes in concentration of trace impurities, the minerals present, and where the trace impurities are located in the structure of the minerals. Thus the method has wide application in determining or observing a variety of differences in mineral grains that otherwise appear similar.

Electron Microscopes

Electron microscopes have proved very useful in forensic work because it is possible to examine particles at very high magnifications, thus bringing out details that would otherwise not be seen. The *Transmission Electron Microscope* (TEM) permits study of objects as small as 2 Angstrom units, from about 200× to 250,000×. With this instrument it is only possible to examine the surface of a particle by means of a replica. The surface of the particle is usually coated with carbon and the particle removed. It is the carbon replica or coating that is viewed with the microscope. Preparing replicas of minerals and related particles is somewhat difficult and time consuming. In addition, the coating may be imperfect and only part of the surface useful for study. Preparation of the sample normally results in destruction of the original particle. Despite these problems the instrument may be useful where ultrahigh magnifications are needed.

The *scanning electron microscope* (SEM) has a wide range of magnifications, generally from 15× to over 50,000× and can record something as small as 200 Angstrom units. This instrument became commercially available in the mid-1960's and has been rapidly introduced in forensic work especially in the study of hair, fibers, paint, and various very small particles. It has the advantage that the surface of a sample may be viewed directly. However, an ultrathin coating of gold plated on the specimen improves the quality of the picture. The depth of field is very large and most SEM pictures have an excellent three-dimensional appearance. In using the instrument it is possible to change magnification easily and thus study the appearance of the surface from very low to very high magnification. Differences in very small fossils that were not previously known can now be seen during routine examination. Surface features of individual grains of minerals such as quartz can be seen and

shown to have many different kinds of scratches (Fig. 7-8). Some
of these scratches may be useful in telling us the past history of
the individual grain. It is not uncommon to observe other minerals such as clay flakes filling the scratches and thus adding
another characteristic that can be useful in comparing the minerals.

When using these powerful instruments in forensic work, it
is well to keep in mind that no two objects are ever exactly the
same. No two sand grains are ever exactly alike when studied

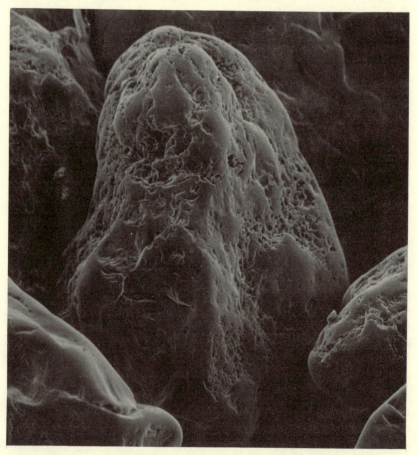

Figure 7-8   A single quartz sand grain as seen through a scanning electron
microscope. *Courtesy of Robert Holzer*

under the high magnifications of an electron microscope. This is true even if they have been side by side for the past million years. Observations made with these instruments can be very useful for establishing comparison or lack of comparison between samples. However, the very power of the instruments permits the possibility of their abuse in the hands of the unscrupulous. If we were to do a complete chemical analysis of a total person, by the most modern methods, in the morning and repeat the analysis on the same person in the afternoon, we would find chemical differences. However, this would not demonstrate that we had analyzed two different people. Thus the demonstration of small differences in soil does not prove in itself that they do not compare. It is equally true that showing a common similarity among soil samples, such as their both containing quartz, is poor evidence on which to base a comparison. The professional judgment of the scientist thus becomes increasingly important when these powerful instruments are used.

Micromorphology

Micromorphology (from the Greek meaning a study of the small forms) is a study of the detailed features of minerals, soils, organic materials and other substances and in particular how one part relates to another. It could be considered a specialized branch of petrography in that the petrographic microscope is used extensively in investigations. The petrographer thin-sections a rock for microscopic examination and in so doing is able to see how one mineral relates to another under natural conditions. Soils laboratories for the most part utilize a somewhat different approach for conventional chemical and mineralogical analyses in which a soil sample is sieved, mixed —and in some cases ground—prior to analysis. In this process the total composition of the sample remains unchanged but the relation of one part to another is lost. If one were to identify a sample of wood he would look at its grain and study it using microscopic techniques, or still better he would prefer to examine the living tree so that he could study its form, shape, and other natural features. On the other hand, if a specimen of wood were reduced to sawdust, in many cases it would be quite difficult to make positive identification as to the type of tree the wood came from. Micromorphology utilizes the concept of studying the natural fabric of the soil with a minimum of disturbance of the sample. One can isolate a grain of silt and determine its mineral and chemical composition, but what is equally or even more important is its position, function, and relation to other matter within the soil system. By comparative morphology one can show similarities or dissimilarities between samples. Two different soil samples may contain equal percentages of clay and thus physical composition would show great similarity, but such an analysis would not show whether the clay was present as aggregates, as clay coatings on the larger particles, or whether it was evenly distributed throughout the matrix.

Techniques for sample preparation and analysis involve collecting a sample of geologic or soil material with as little disturbance as possible so that the structural properties remain unaltered. After collection and drying, the sample is impregnated with a plastic and allowed to harden. The block of material is then sawed into slices which are then ground and mounted on a glass slide and polished in a manner similar to thin-sectioning rock specimens. The thin section can then be studied as to content, nature, and weathering of minerals. Also plant parts can be identified in a similar manner.

X-ray Diffraction

X-ray diffraction is one of the most important and reliable methods of identifying the composition of geologic, soil, and other crystalline substances. The method is based on the arrangement of atoms, ions, and molecules within the specimen. The sample is analyzed by passing X-rays through a crystal and measuring the angle of the diffracted X-rays (Fig. 7-9). Each crystalline material has its own distinctive X-ray pattern. Figure 7-9 shows an X-ray beam impinging on a specimen and then being diffracted. The principle is based on the Bragg law: $n\lambda = 2d \sin \theta$ in which n is the order of reflection, λ is the wave length of the X-ray beam, d is the lattice spacing within the

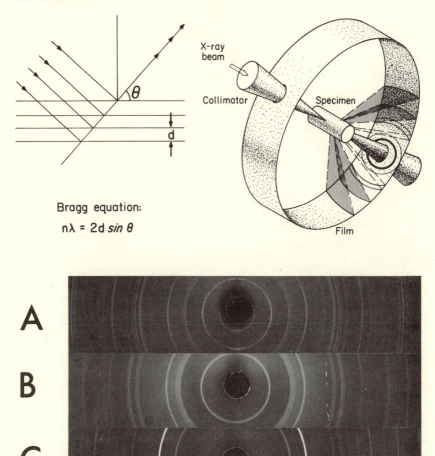

Bragg equation:

$$n\lambda = 2d\,\sin\theta$$

Figure 7-9   The principles of X-ray diffraction are based on the Bragg equation. The upper left diagram depicts X-rays of a certain wave length (λ) penetrating a crystal. Distance between two adjacent planes is shown as d and n is an integer. The reflected X-ray beam is shown as θ. The upper right diagram shows an X-ray powder camera. The specimen is rotated in the center of the camera and the X-ray pattern forms on the film lining the camera housing. The lower part of the figure shows X-ray powder photographs of three minerals (*A*) chlorite, (*B*) kaolinite and (*C*) quartz.

crystal and θ is the glancing angle of reflection. Figure 7-9 shows reflected X-ray beams with various spacings and intensities recorded on photographic film. The diffraction pattern of a sample is controlled by the internal structure of the specimen. The diffraction pattern can be recorded more accurately (and easily if sufficient sample is available) by use of a diffractometer to pick up the pulses and record them on a print-out. The interpretation of X-ray patterns under normal situations is a comparatively simple matter. Two factors are of prime importance in the interpretation: the d-spacing from d in the Bragg law which is expressed in Angstroms $[(\text{Å}) (1 \times 10^{-8} \text{ cm or } 0.0039$ millionths of an inch)$]$, and the intensity. After the diffractogram is made and lines are measured their intensities approximated thus:

QUARTZ		CALCITE	
d (Å)	Intensity	d (Å)	Intensity
3.34	v. stg.	3.04	v. stg.
4.26	mod.	2.29	wk.
1.82	wk.	2.10	wk.

There are at least two avenues for interpreting X-ray diffractograms: The first involves measuring the d values and intensities and comparing this information with published lists of data on minerals. The second involves comparing the X-ray pattern directly with the pattern produced by a known mineral. If a comparison between samples is to be made there are situations in which the X-ray diffractograms themselves may be compared without actual identification of the substance.

Among the strong points favoring the use of X-ray diffraction patterns is that they record the crystal structure. If two substances, diamond and graphite, were analyzed chemically they would be identical because both are composed of pure carbon, but X-ray diffractograms of the two minerals would be quite different. Many samples are mixtures of two or more substances. If substances are analyzed chemically some difficulties may be encountered because the actual chemical form of the substances at times cannot be established. As an example, we can use a mixture of two salts, sodium chloride and potassium nitrate. If the composition of the sample were determined by the usual chemical methods it would reveal sodium, potassium, chloride and nitrate—but what were the original compounds? Were they sodium chloride and potassium nitrate or were they sodium nitrate and potassium chloride or a mixture of four salts? An X-ray diffractogram of such a salt mixture would tell us specifically the form of the salt.

X-ray diffraction is used as the principal tool in modern identification of clay minerals. Chemical composition of clays generally tells us very little as to the nature of clay substances, but the possibilities of identification of clays by X-ray diffraction are almost unlimited. Clays as well as other crystalline substances can be X-rayed and if identification is desired the composition of the sample can be ascertained by measuring the diffraction patterns from a standard reference book or from reference cards.*

In order to better acquaint the reader with the appearance of X-ray diffractograms Figure 7-10 lists a commonly accepted pattern of a reference and that of a soil clay. It is important to point out, however, that even a trace of contamination within a sample may produce a somewhat different pattern. For example, Figure 7-10 shows an X-ray diffractogram of a relatively pure sample of kaolinite. After a single grain of quartz was ground and mixed (with a resulting ratio of 99 parts kaolinite and 1 part quartz), this sample was X-rayed. The pattern showed a significant change—a characteristic introduced by a single quartz grain.

X-ray diffraction studies can be made on any crystalline material. The problem of X-raying organic substances such as plant parts or plant extracts, however, is quite involved and should be carried out only by highly skilled professionals.

Mineral samples may be X-rayed as a complete sample or they may be fractionated according to size and/or density and the fractions analyzed and compared.

* Perhaps the most complete information is found in the *Index to the X-ray Powder Data File* and the cards themselves published by the American Society for Testing Materials, 1916 Race St., Philadelphia, Pa.

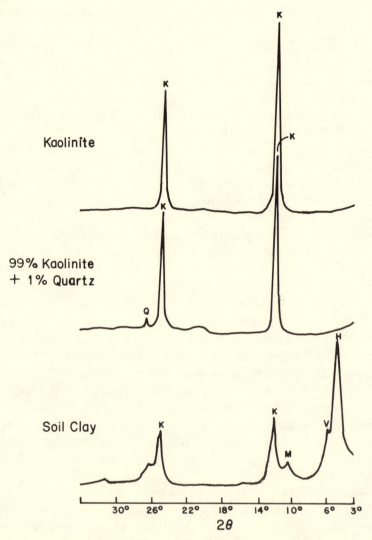

Figure 7-10 Comparative diffractograms of kaolinite, kaolinite with quartz, and soil clay.

If sands from many sources are X-rayed, the patterns may appear to be very similar or virtually identical. This is because quartz and to some extent feldspar usually make up the bulk of the material. In such instances it would be more definitive to isolate the heavy minerals, grind them to a powder, and make diffractograms for comparison.

Differential Thermal Analysis

Differential thermal analysis can be used successfully as an analytical technique for making comparisons between various geologic and ceramic materials, soil, soaps, organic acids, polymers, foods, coal, rubber, and many other materials. The principle involves either the absorption or the release of heat as a sample is heated continuously over a range of temperatures. The material to be identified is heated in a specially designed furnace in which the temperature can be raised at a constant rate from room temperature to about 1000° C. Two samples are heated simultaneously in the furnace. One is a reference sample consisting of inert material which does not undergo a thermal reaction when heated and the other the sample to be identified. The two specimens are placed in the furnace and the unknown will, upon heating, undergo a series of reactions—dehydration, decomposition, crystalline transformation, melting, boiling, and others. Some of these reactions give off heat and are referred to as *exothermic* whereas others take on heat and are referred to as *endothermic* reactions. Thermocouples are embedded in the samples (or the sample holders can be constructed to serve as thermocouples) and the temperature differences (Δ) between the two samples determined (Fig. 7-11). The temperature differences between the sample and the reference material are plotted as functions of increasing temperature. A straight base line indicates no temperature differential, which in turn reflects chemical and physical stability of the sample. Peaks or valleys deflected from the base line, however, indicate reactions at certain temperature ranges. Not only is it important to record the temperature at which the endothermic or exothermic reaction occurs but also the intensity of the reaction. After various sam-

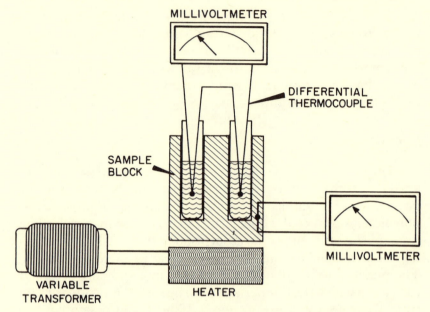

Figure 7-11 Diagram of differential thermal analysis apparatus.

ples are analyzed by differential thermal techniques the graphs can be compared qualitatively and to an extent quantitatively (Fig. 7-12). Most samples in nature will contain a mixture of materials and a single thermograph may contain a series of peaks and valleys which may have been contributed by various materials.

With certain compounds it is desirable to use a controlled atmosphere in the furnace. Many organic compounds, upon decomposition, liberate a relatively large amount of heat, but if such samples are heated in the presence of a gas such as nitrogen, the heat is simply absorbed during sample decomposition.

In interpretating thermograms, one method is to identify the compounds by locating the temperature and intensity of the various reactions and comparing them with published standards.

For comparative purposes in forensic science thermograms may be superposed over one another for observing similarities or differences.

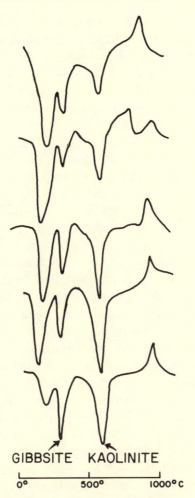

GIBBSITE   KAOLINITE

0°   500°   1000° C

Figure 7-12   Differential thermograms of clay taken at various depths in a soil. The top thermogram is from the surface soil and the lower thermograms show clay from progressively deeper layers within the soil. The clay consists primarily of gibbsite and kaolinite. (Unpublished data of W. H. Farley.)

Chemical Methods

From time to time data from a "soil analysis" are used for forensic purposes. Such an expression suggests officialdom. In many cases a soil analysis is assumed to be a determination of the chemical components of the soil. A review of many court cases where soil, sediment, or rock (chemical) analyses have been introduced in evidence would leave the forensic geologist with mixed feelings in that in some situations the analyses and data interpretation are valid, but in others they are open to serious criticism. In a court case involving murder in a small eastern town a comparison was made between samples of soil from the site where a murder victim was found and the mud caked under the fenders of the suspect's automobile. The fine fractions were sieved and ignited, and it was found that they all turned a brilliant red color. From this color comparison between the sets of samples it was stated that there was a positive comparison between the two sets of samples. Such a comparison has as much validity as saying that two steaks came from the same carcass because after grilling both turned a brown color. In Chapter 4, type examples of major and trace soil elemental composition are given. Since the terms "soil analysis" and "soil composition" in themselves specify neither the type of analysis nor the methodology, more information must be supplied before final appraisal of the data can be made.

Before the advent of modern instruments, soil and geologic samples were generally analyzed chemically by rather long and tedious methods, commonly referred to as *wet chemical* methods. These methods are described in a number of publications and most procedures are still considered acceptable. The work of Piper (1947), Bear (1964), and the "Methods of Analysis" published usually every five years in book form by the Association of Official Analytical Chemists,* have for many years served as authoritative references. During the last quarter-century there have been revolutionary changes in methods used in soil and rock analyses and the larger, modern laboratories now have many sophisticated instruments and accordingly new methods have been introduced. These modern instruments are used in data gathering such as the identification of elements, compounds, and minerals.

The following pages serve as an introduction to certain instruments and methods used in establishing the chemical iden-

---

* See reference in Chapter 4.

tity of materials. As such, the discussions are brief outlines of the principles involved and by no means imply procedural details.

Chemical analyses of soils, sediments, and rocks may be carried out by a number of procedures. Although there is no one method without certain limitations, there are a number of available methods that are considered satisfactory. A number of reference books are published on analytical procedures which cover theory as well as methodology (Piper, 1947; Jackson, 1958; Bear, 1964; Black, 1965; and others).

Fusion Analysis

This is a classical method used for the determination of the major soil constituents in soils and minerals—particularly Si, Fe, Al, Ca, Mg, Ti, P and others (Piper, 1947). The method consists of fusing a ground sample with Na_2CO_3 at which time the sample will actually go into solution. Then by differential solubilities certain elements can be precipitated out or determined gravimetrically or by colorimetric procedures.

Silica/Sesquioxide Ratios

The silica-sesquioxide ratios of clay minerals give some general information about their nature but such information cannot be assumed to be highly specific. The sesquioxides which consist of Fe_2O_3 plus Al_2O_3 are designated as the R_2O_3 group. In some instances TiO_2, MnO and P_2O_5 are also included within the R_2O_3 group. The SiO_2/R_2O_3 ratio may be of considerable value in establishing whether a clay has undergone a high degree of mineral and chemical alteration or wether it has been merely reduced in size mechanically. The SiO_2/R_2O_3 ratio is calculated by dividing the formula weights by molecular weights and expressing the values as a ratio, for example:

$$\frac{\dfrac{\%\ SiO_2}{60.3}}{\dfrac{\%\ Fe_2O_3}{159.7} + \dfrac{\%\ Al_2O_3}{102.0}} = X$$

A value of 4 would indicate 4 units of silica to 1 of the R_2O_3 group. Values of less than 2 indicate a high degree of mineral and chemical alteration. Except in special situations the SiO_2/R_2O_3 ratio would not be considered diagnostic because most values fall within the 2 to 4 range.

In addition to SiO_2/R_2O_3 ratios some investigators consider the SiO_2/Al_2O_3 color ratios of clays. Such criteria have approximately the same importance as do the SiO_2/R_2O_3 ratios.

Moisture

In some situations it is necessary to determine the amount of moisture in a sample. This is particularly true with clays or peats. A known weight of the soil sample is heated in a tared weighing bottle to 105–110° C. for about ten hours, cooled, and reweighed. The loss of weight is reported as moisture. Because of the nature of forensic samples, it is seldom that this value is significant.

Igniting Soil Samples for Comparison

Occasionally forensic laboratories ignite soil samples at temperatures ranging from 500°–1000° C. and make color comparisons of the ignited materials. The purpose of this procedure is to destroy the organic matter in the sample so that an examination can be made of the residual mineral colors, which are usually some shade of red, orange, yellow, brown, etc. Such a procedure may be helpful in some situations but as a general rule it tends to create false impressions. The main limitation in the heating procedure is that while the elevated temperatures destroy the organic residues, the iron in the sample is converted to an oxidized state which results in a reddish color. Many samples of completely different origin may appear to be identical after the ignition treatment.

If it is desirable to make a comparison between samples with the organic matter removed, it is more realistic to destroy the organic matter with hydrogen peroxide rather than by heat. The process has to be repeated with samples high in organic matter.

Even though the peroxide may alter some minerals, the color comparison should be considered more valid than that from ignited samples.

Loss on Ignition

The moisture-free sample is heated to 700° C. for one-half hour. The loss of weight is reported as percent ignition loss. This value represents organic matter plus tightly held water.

Organic Matter

About 58 percent of the organic matter in the soil is in the form of organic carbon. Therefore, the percentage of organic carbon in a sample is multiplied by the factor 1.72 to approximate the percentage of organic matter. The two methods used for determining organic carbon are:
    1. Wet oxidation of the organic carbon with chromic acid.
    2. Dry combustion by heating the sample and trapping the evolved CO_2 in an absorbent.
    The total amount of organic matter in a soil seldom has evidential value.

Instrumental Methods of Analyses

There are a number of instrumental methods now available for making chemical analyses of mineral material.
    X-ray fluorescence spectrometry is used for elemental determination of a wide range of materials. The principle involves the bombardment of the sample with a high-energy primary X-ray beam and each element, when excited by the X-rays, emits secondary X-rays which are recorded (Vanden Heuvel, 1965). The method, in addition to being used for soil and rock samples, can also be applied to many other materials such as glass, paint, brick, paper, water and others (Fig. 7-13) (Wood and Mathieson, 1973).
    Emission spectrography is a method used for simultaneous determination of most elemental components of rocks or soils

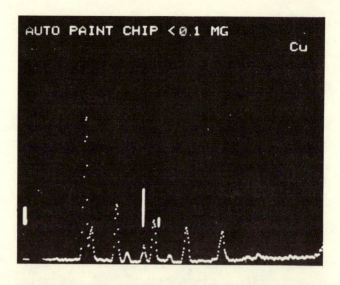

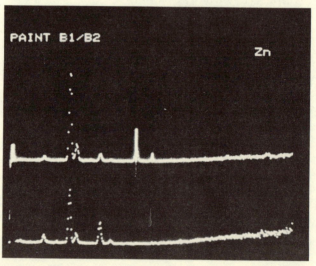

Figure 7-13 Elemental analysis of materials using X-ray spectroscopy techniques. *A*, oscilloscope display of spectrum from automobile paint chip. K$_\alpha$ and K$_\beta$ lines of copper illustrated; *B*, overlapped spectra of two paint chips. Zinc K$_\alpha$ and K$_\beta$ lines identified. *Courtesy of Finnigan Corp.*

(Specht, Myers, and Oda, 1965). The sample is fired in a graphite electrode at a high temperature and light is emitted as a result of excitation of atoms. Recordings are made on a photographic plate or direct reading instruments. Usually determinations for Si, Fe, and Al are more accurate using the classic wet chemical methods but most other elements, particularly the trace metals, are readily determined by such spectrographic techniques.

Atomic Absorption Spectrophotometry

Atomic absorption spectrophotometry is a reliable method for estimating the concentration of certain elements in rock, mineral, and soil samples. It consists of measuring the absorption of radiation in the atomic vapor produced from the sample at a wave length that is specific and characteristic for the element. Basically the instrument consists of (1) a primary source of radiation, (2) equipment for producing atomic vapor, (3) a wave-length selector, (4) a radiation detector, and (5) a read-out unit.

Small samples—generally one gram or less—are first heated by fusing them with Na_2CO_3 so that the specimen can be placed into solution. A relatively wide range of elements such as K, Ca, Mg, Al, Fe, Mn and a number of trace metals can be determined by this method.

Infrared Spectrometry

Infrared spectrometry is used as a technique for identifying both inorganic as well as organic materials. The principle involved is the determination of the bonding energy of molecules and ions within specified regions of the light spectrum. Materials subjected to radiation will absorb radiation frequencies characteristic of the sample, which are then recorded on a chart (Fig. 7-14), usually the 2–20 micron wave-length region is used. A compound having a known structure yields a characteristic pattern and from this "fingerprint" method absorption bands are assigned to functional groups (e.g., phenol or carbonate). The

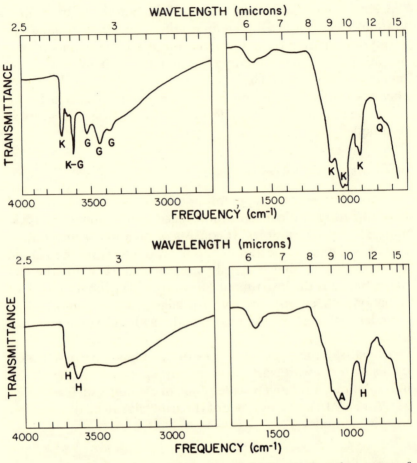

Figure 7-14   Infrared spectra of clay materials. *Above,* infrared spectrum of clay fraction of a Columbian soil formed on unconsolidated sediments (K = kaolinite; G = gibbsite; Q = quartz). *Below,* infrared spectrum of the clay of a Columbian soil formed from volcanic ash (H = hallosite; A = allophane). *Courtesy of J. L. White and Soil Science*

use of infrared absorption techniques is receiving wide acceptance in the identification of organic as well as inorganic substances. Most studies involving organic materials, however, are by comparison techniques. In only a few cases are the compounds totally identified. Instead certain structures within the compounds are recorded. These structures may be from ammonia, carboxyl, and various aromatic sulfates and phosphates. There are fairly comprehensive lists available which list the wave lengths assigned to various substances, for example:

Wave Length μ	Wave Number cm^{-1}	Assignment
6.85	1460	$CC\text{-}H_3$
11.36–12.50	880–800	CO_3^{2-} vibrations
9.65–10.00	1037–1000	PO_4^{3-} vibrations

Information is available from the standpoint of the position of the absorption bands of many compounds and groups. Valuable quantitative measurements may be also derived from intensity measurements.

Infrared absorption techniques usually cannot be considered conclusive in the identification of geologic and soil samples but they can be considered reliable methods for comparison of samples.

Neutron Activation Analysis

Neutron activation analysis has been used in science where elemental composition of samples has been required. This is a nondestructive instrumental method and uses only a small sample. It is a gamma ray spectrometric procedure in which a soil or rock sample is irradiated in a thermal neutron flux and the induced radionuclides measured. A complete analysis of all elements cannot be made by neutron activation, therefore certain elements are generally selected as tracers such as manganese, sodium, and barium. High concentrations of certain elements in the soil or rock samples may serve as reliable tracers but on the other hand the high concentration of certain elements may blot out the spectra of other elements; for this reason it is often desirable to use some form of a complementary analysis such as atomic absorption or emission spectrography.

In a case involving the transport of 2400 gallons of illegal whiskey from Georgia to New York, the soil material recovered from the tractor trailer in New York was studied in comparison with soils collected from the location of an illegal still in Georgia. A similarity of the two sets of samples based on similar chemical analysis by neutron activation was submitted in evidence during the trial.

Ion Exchange

Soils and geologic materials have capacity for adsorbing certain materials from solution. The reaction involves both positively charged ions (cations)—particularly H^+, Ca^{2+}, Mg^{2+}, Na^+, and K^+—and negatively charged ions (anions), such as PO_4^{3-}, SO_4^{2-}, and Cl with the surfaces of mineral and organic particles. A soil or geologic material with the capacity for adsorbing large quantities of cations or anions would be characterized as having a large exchange capacity and vice versa. Two factors of special importance in ion exchange studies are (1) the *capacity* of the soil to adsorb ions and (2) *composition* or ratios of the adsorbed ions.

It would be entirely possible for comparative purposes to consider the cation exchange capacity of materials. This is usually carried out by determining the amount of material adsorbed on the exchange complex. For example, if a soil were leached with ammonium acetate and the excess ammonium removed, that ammonium retained on the material would represent the cation exchange capacity. Values are generally expressed quantitatively as milliequivalents (me.) per 100 grams of material. Cation exchange capacities generally will range from lows of 1–3 to highs of 30 to 50 milliequivalents (me.) per 100 grams. Clay, especially that of the montmorillonite type, has a high exchange capacity as does organic matter, whereas sands have a low exchange capacity.

In addition to the capacity of the soil or geologic material to adsorb cations is the problem of the saturating cations themselves. The bulk of cations on the exchange complex generally consists of calcium, magnesium, sodium, potassium, aluminum and hydrogen. Therefore, one may make a comparison of the saturating cations on various samples. The degree of importance that can be ascribed to the comparison of cation exchange data among samples is problematical. Normally cation exchange data would not be considered to have significant evidential value except in special situations.

Fertilizer and Spray Residue Detection

Cultivated fields and gardens are often fertilized and limed as well as sprayed with insecticides, fungicides, and herbicides. Some of the added materials may leach from the soil or degrade biologically, but there are usually residues partially persisting for some years after application. If ground limestone is added to the soil some of the calcite or dolomite may persist for at least several years. Fertilizers added to the soil generally consist of nitrogen, phosphorus, and potash with perhaps some trace elements. Potash and especially nitrogen leach from the soil rather rapidly but the phosphorus is less soluble and tends to build up in the soil. In the heavily fertilized vegetable soils in eastern North America, it is common to have five times as much "available" phosphorus as in the unfertilized wooded sectors. In a situation where a person was charged with stealing potatoes from another man's field, it was found that the superphosphate in the soil clinging to the potatoes was matched to that of the soil in the field from which the theft occurred. Other possibilities exist with respect to spray residues such as copper sulphate (no longer extensively used) and various organic additives. The copper content of a soil may increase as much as five-fold through the use of copper-containing sprays. Insecticides such as DDT and lindane may build up in the soil and some 75 percent of the application will generally persist after it is in the soil for one year.

Organic Comparisons

This volume primarily concerns rocks, minerals, and soils and there is only a small amount of attention focusing on organic complexes in the soil. The potential for using organic compounds in soils for forensic purposes is promising, but developments have been few. In addition to determining the total quantity of organic substances including humus in the soil, many of the organic compounds can also be determined individually. Thornton (1973) reviewed the possibilities of using certain organic compounds in soils for identification purposes. Among those subjects considered are carbohydrates, hydrocarbons, ketones, lipids, amino acids, organic phosphorus and organic sulfur compounds, enzymes, among others present. Organic compounds in the soil will generally vary between soil types and there may be long-term effects as well as seasonal changes at any one site reflecting the time of year and climatic conditions. Once a sample is stored there may be decomposition of certain organic compounds, but the order of magnitude may not necessarily be great. For example, enzyme activity may be decreased upon drying of the soil, but subsequent changes are of a comparatively low order. The forensic scientist must realize that certain sets of properties in the soil such as silt content and mineral content are largely permanent ones, but many of those of an organic nature are transitory.

Conductivity

Conductivity is a measurement of an electrical current through a soil or soil extract from which is calculated the percentage of soluble salt present. In desert regions, coastal sectors, and in natural brines the amount of soluble salt present may be used for forensic comparison. The greater the percentage of salt present, the greater will be the conductivity. Conductivity readings do not tell the type of salt present—only the approximate quantity. There are two general methods used for conductivity determinations, (1) placing soil in a hard rubber or plastic cup with electrodes; the mineral material is saturated with water and a current is passed between the electrodes and the conductance (Ec) which is expressed in *mhos* (*Soil Survey Handbook*, 1951), and (2) extracting the salt from the sample with water and determining the conductivity of the leachate (Richards, 1954). The following is a guide for comparing salt content to conductivity:

$Ec \times 10^3$	Pct. Salt
5	0.08
10	0.17
20	0.36
30	0.55
40	0.76
50	0.96

Soil Acidity

The degree of acidity (or alkalinity) of soils and geologic materials is expressed in pH values, which in effect is a measure of the free hydrogen ion concentration in solution. The greater the quantity of H ions present, the greater the degree of acidity. Technically, the acidity is expressed in pH values which range from about 0 to 14 with lower values indicating greater acidity. pH is defined as the negative logarithm of the hydrogen ions in solution. The pH values of soils generally range from 3.5 to 8.5 or possibly higher. Soils in eastern United States are usually leached of their more soluble constituents and accordingly will have a strongly acid reaction ranging from 3.8 to 5.5. Farther west where precipitation is less, the pH values will be somewhat higher—approximating 5 to 6.5 and in the desert regions they are still higher—approximating 6 to 8.0 or even higher. These stated values must be considered only as a general guide and there are many local exceptions. For example, limestone soils in the eastern United States have pH values as high as 8 at a depth of two to four feet. Also in the alkali regions of the Far West the pH values of the soils will be above 8 because of the alkali present. In the vicinity of smelters, power plants, and other industrial areas using coal the pH values may be very low —sometimes less than 3. In some situations there are sulfur-bearing minerals in the soil which cause abnormally low pH values.

It is somewhat of an open question as to how much forensic importance can be attached to the pH value of a soil or geologic

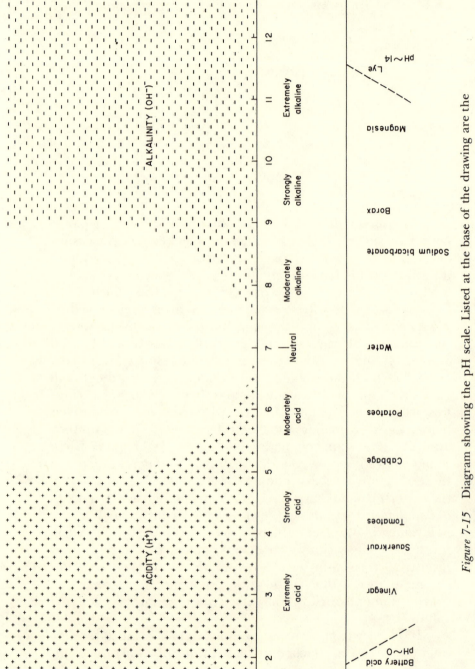

Figure 7-15 Diagram showing the pH scale. Listed at the base of the drawing are the approximate pH values of some common materials.

sample, but where extreme values are present such information may be successfully used to indicate possible origin.

In Japan a four-foot soil auger has been successfully used to find bodies that had been buried several months prior to the search. The soil collected on the auger is tested with litmus paper for a strong alkaline reaction. Decomposition of a body produces in the final stage alkaline substances which permeate the surrounding soil. In earlier stages of decomposition an acid reaction would be expected. The specific location to be searched has sometimes been determined by study of soil on objects that were believed to be on the scene at the time of the burial. Once these soil samples had been studied it was possible to outline possible areas where similar types of soils exist thus limiting the number of possible areas to be searched and probed.

Iron Staining of Particles (reducible iron or free oxides of iron)

Iron staining of soils and geologic material is a well-known condition. The red, brown, and yellowish coloration usually results from iron being in an altered and oxidized form. In general it can be stated that the amount of iron staining (reducible iron or free oxides of iron) present depends largely upon climate, age, site, and the material itself. The older, well-drained positions tend to have more reddish colors reflecting advanced weathering. In comparative analysis it is not only important to determine mineral species, but also to consider the amount of iron staining on the particles as well. Thus a feldspar particle may be identified as such, but if there is iron staining present, such ancillary information would be a critical added criterion.

The amount of reducible iron in geologic or soil material can be determined chemically (Kilmer, 1960). The quantity of reducible iron in a sample may be as high as 20 percent or more, but with most samples, values are much lower. Within any sample the clay fraction will generally have larger amounts of reducible iron than will the coarse fractions. Therefore, if any quantification is made it is critical to consider geologic and soil fractions within the same size range.

Oxidation-Reduction Potentials

Oxidation-reduction potentials, commonly referred to as redox potentials (Eh), may be measured for any soil or sediment (Hesse, 1972). Redox potential is determined by placing a platinum electrode and a reference electrode into the soil and measuring the millivolts between them with suitable equipment. In effect, the principle is one of electron transfer in which during oxidation there is a loss of electrons and during reduction there is a gain of electrons, for example:

$$\text{Oxidized state} + \text{electrons} \rightleftharpoons \text{reduced state}$$

A well-drained site will have a higher redox potential whereas a waterlogged site will have a lower value—often negative.

A number of factors determine the redox potential of a soil: Water-logged soils naturally are oxygen-deficient and hence have a low redox potential. On the other hand, soils that are well aerated tend to have a high redox potential. When organic matter is added to a soil, oxygen is utilized during the organic matter decomposition, which results in a reduction environment. Other factors such as pH, mineral composition, and temperature also influence redox systems but moisture content and organic matter supply are generally the most critical ones. Measurements of Eh values in soils will generally show a range from -0.3 to $+0.4$ volts with the more favorable oxidizing conditions giving higher values. In soils having an oxidized surface soil but with a water table at depth will show a decrease in Eh with increased depth. Eh values of any one site may vary from week to week and should be considered as a changing property, thus this property has use in only limited circumstances.

References

Bear, F. E., ed. 1964. *Chemistry of the soil.* American Chemical Society Monograph, No. 160. New York: Reinhold Publishing Co.

Black, C. A., ed. 1965. *Methods of soil analysis.* Monograph No. 9, Parts 1 and 2. Madison, Wisc.: American Society of Agronomy.

Brown, J. L., and Johnson, J. W. 1973. Electronic microscopy and

X-ray microanalysis in forensic science. *Jour. Assoc. Off. Analytical Chem.* 56:930–943.

Cobb, P. G. W. 1968. A survey of the variations in the physical properties of glass. *Jour. Forensic Sci.* 8:29.

Frenkel, O. J. 1965. A program of research into the value of evidence from southern Ontario soils. *Proc. Can. Soc. Forensic Sci.* Vol. 4, p. 23.

——. 1968. Three studies on the forensic comparison of soil samples. Paper read at 1968 meeting of the American Academy of Forensic Sciences, Chicago, Ill.

Graham, D. 1973. *The use of X-ray techniques in forensic investigations.* London: Churchill Livingston Co.

Herzog, L. F., Marshall, D. J., Babione, R. F. 1970. *The Luminoscope—a New Instrument for Studying the Electron-Stimulated Luminescence of Terrestrial, Extra-Terrestrial and Synthetic Materials under the Microscope, Pennsylvania State University:* MRL Special Publication 70-101, pp. 79–98.

Hesse, P. R. 1972. *A textbook of soil chemical analysis.* New York: Chemical Publishing Co.

Hoffman, C. M., Brunelle, R. I., and Snow, K. B. 1969. Forensic comparisons of soils by neutron activation and atomic absorption analysis. *Jour. Criminal Law, Criminology and Police Science* 60:395–401.

Hughes, D. J. 1958. *The neutron story.* New York: Doubleday & Company.

Jackson, M. L. 1958. *Soil chemical analysis.* Englewood Cliffs, N.J.: Prentice-Hall, Inc.

Kilmer, V. J., and Alexander, L. T. 1949. Methods of making mechanical analyses of soils. *Soil Sci.* 68:15–24.

Kilmer, V. J. 1960. The estimation of free iron oxides in soils. *Soil Sci. Soc. Amer. Proc.* 24:420–421.

Kirk, P. L. 1953. *Crime investigation.* New York: Interscience Publishers, Inc.

Lepper, H. A. 1945. *Official and tentative methods of analysis of the association of official agricultural chemists.* Washington, D.C.: Assoc. Official Anal. Chemists.

McCrone, W. C., and Delly, J. G. 1973. *The particle atlas,* vols. 1–4. Ann Arbor, Mich.: Ann Arbor Science Publishers.

Nickolls, L. C. 1962. Identification of stains of nonbiological origin, in *Methods of forensic science,* Vol. 1, Frank Lundquist, ed. New York: Interscience Publishers.

Ojena, S. M., and Deforest, P. R. 1972. Precise refractive index determination of the immersion method, using phase contrast microscopy and the Mettler hot stage. *Jour. Forensic Sci.* 12:315–329.

Piper, C. S. 1947. *Soil and plant analysis.* New York: Interscience Publishers, Inc.

Rees, P. O. 1968. The determination and the comparison of the refractive index of glass fragments by means of a temperature control method. *Jour. Forensic Sci.* 8:25.

Smale, D., and Trueman, N. A. 1969. Heavy mineral studies as evidence in a murder case in outback Australia. *Jour. Forensic Sci. Soc.* 9:3, 4.

Smale, David. 1973. The examination of paint flakes, glass and soils for forensic purposes, with special reference to electron probe microanalysis. *Jour. Forensic Sci. Soc.* 13:5.

Thornton, J. I. 1974. Forensic biochemical characterization of soils. Ph.D. thesis, University of California, Berkeley.

Vanden Heuvel, R. C. 1965. Elemental analysis of X-ray emission spectrography in methods of soil analysis. Monograph No. 9, V. 2 (C. A. Black, ed.). American Society of Agronomy, Madison, Wisc., Paper No. 52.

Wiklander, L. 1964. *Cation and anion exchange phenomena in chemistry of the soil* (F. E. Bear, ed.). New York: Reinhold Publishing Co.

Winchell, A. N., and Winchell, H. 1964. *The microscopical character of artificial inorganic solid substances.* New York and London: Academic Press.

Wood, W., and Mathieson, J. 1973. *The elemental fingerprint in pollution and criminalistic applications.* Finnegan Spectra 3, No. 2.

8 Application of Geologic Information and Instruments

Most of the examples and methods we have discussed have involved, in one way or another, the application of techniques of comparison. The principle underlying these studies has been the usefulness of data obtained from associated or questioned samples when these data are compared with other information or data from control samples. The purpose of these studies is to contribute scientific evidence that helps to establish guilt or innocence of an individual with respect to a certain criminal act or to provide assistance during an investigation that will provide a clue or help establish responsibility in criminal or civil matters.

In this chapter we will examine some additional tools and methods of geology and soil science that have been applied or might be applied to special forensic problems. In some of these examples the investigator faced with a problem that involves the earth or earth materials recognizes that geology or earth science might make a contribution and approaches an earth scientist with the problem. There are undoubtedly many possibilities other than the ones examined here, and new examples appear each year. They appear when a problem faced by the skilled, imaginative, dedicated investigator is brought to the attention of a like-minded scientist. With these types of cases it is well to

165

remember that the particular methods used in one case may not necessarily be useful in all similar cases.

One of the main reasons for this section is to bring together in an organized fashion some of these examples, so that the ideas will be available to the investigator and the scientist in the hope that the "wheel will not have to be invented again" in each case.

Geophysical Methods

Many instruments have been developed and are available that give us information about the kinds of rocks, their shape and inclinations under the surface of the earth. These have proved to be of great value in the search for minerals, oil, and gas. Such geophysical instruments measure properties of rocks beneath the surface of the earth and permit us to identify or predict what will be found beneath the surface.

The *magnetometer* is an instrument that measures variations in the strength of the earth's magnetic field. There are various types of magnetometers, such as the magnetic balance, fluxgate magnetometer, and nuclear resonance magnetometer. Magnetic field intensity is measured in *oersteds*. The term *gauss* is also used and is numerically equivalent. The total magnetic field of the earth, that is, the field that causes a common compass to point toward the north magnetic pole, has a strength of approximately 0.5 oersteds. In most work the measurement is recorded in *gammas,* which is defined as 1/10,000th of an oersted. Magnetic balance instruments commonly can measure differences in the intensity of the earth's magnetic field of one or two gammas. Similar accuracy is obtained from the fluxgate magnetometers. The natural magnetic intensity of the earth can change several thousand gammas over distances of a few miles because the underlying rocks change. Some rocks have greater magnetic susceptibility than others. In general those rocks with magnetic minerals, such as the mineral magnetite, have the greater susceptibility and thus produce the more intense magnetic readings. Some of the world's most important mines, particularly iron mines, have been discovered by using a magnetometer.

A mass of iron in or on the earth will intensify that natural earth's magnetic field and this intensification, if strong enough, can be detected with a magnetometer. Instruments are now available that can be carried on land, flown in an airplane, or dragged under water by a boat. The earliest use of the airborne magnetometer was in submarine detection during World War II. It was a Fluxgate type and formed the basis of the MAD (Magnetic Airborne Detector) system. The aircraft carrying the instrument flew the oceans and recorded the intensity of the earth's magnetic field. When a submarine, representing a large mass of iron in the sea, was overflown the instrument recorded higher values. Needless to say, there are many other large masses of iron on the bottom of the sea and these were also detected. Experience and careful recording of the location of known sunken ships improved the interpretation and detection of submarines. After the war the instrument was widely used for detection of minerals and also for locating rock structures that might contain oil.

There have been many applications of the magnetometer in forensic work. For example, a few years ago a well-known citizen of a Midwestern town and his new Cadillac automobile disappeared. Within a few months someone remembered having seen the vehicle in the vicinity of an active open pit coal mine. In addition, there was some reason to believe that the missing man had been the possible victim of foul play. In an open pit mine, large volumes of earth are removed from the surface so that the coal that lies several tens or hundreds of feet below the surface can be exposed and removed. The overlying earth is picked up and carried away on giant conveyor belts and dropped in large piles away from the area to be mined. It was suspected that the vehicle, possibly with the victim inside, might have been driven under the unattended end of the conveyor belt and buried. Company records indicated the general area of dumping during the time of the disappearance. However, this included several acres of earth tens of feet thick. A magnetometer survey made on land over the area produced several areas of unusually high magnetic intensity. Prior to the running of the survey an automobile of similar kind was placed in the mine near the edge and measurements were made on the surface above the vehicle.

It was determined that the instrument would easily detect the car even if buried to a depth of up to at least 70 feet. The areas of high magnetic intensity were drilled although none appeared high enough to indicate a mass of iron as large as a car. The drilling and digging uncovered pieces of iron wire. However, the lead proved false and the Cadillac was not found.

Although they operate on several different principles, common metal or mineral detectors have often been used to locate small metal objects, such as firearms, that had been buried just below the surface. These instruments generally must be close to the object in order to detect them and are most useful in locating objects that lie within a few inches or feet of the surface.

The seismograph records vibrations that travel as waves through the rocks of the earth. The geologist uses this method to determine the kinds and distribution of rocks under the surface of the earth. In using the method, two things are necessary: (1) There must be some way of producing a shock wave and (2) some way of detecting the waves after they have traveled through the earth. The waves travel through different kinds of rocks at different velocities. Thus we record the time it takes for the waves to travel from the place of the shock to the place of the detector; and knowing the distance, determine the velocity, and thus something about the rock. The shock may be produced naturally by an earthquake, or artificially by explosives. Small instruments use the shock produced by hitting with a sledge hammer a metal plate placed on the ground. In another method, the explosion is produced at the surface, the waves travel down into the earth, and reflect off rock layers within the earth and return to the surface. We record the total travel time down and back. Knowing the kinds of rocks and the velocity with which the waves travel through them, it is possible to determine the depth below the surface at which the layer of rock that reflected the waves exists. In this way it is possible to find the depth below the surface at which various rocks will be found.

There have been attempts to determine the exact time of an explosion by consulting the records of seismographs that normally record natural earthquakes. Success depends on both the intensity of the blast and the nearness of the recording seismograph. Similar methods are used to record nuclear explosions on a global scale.

The detector that picks up the waves is often called a *geophone*. Geophones form the basis of the *Seismic Intrusion Detection System*. In this system, very sensitive geophones are placed in a perimeter around the area to be protected. They are small boxes with a spike that is pushed into the ground and are usually connected by wire to a recorder. The footstep of a person on the ground is sufficient to cause a small shock wave to travel through the rock or soil and be picked up by the geophone. With present instruments, a person of average weight, walking within thirty to fifty yards of the geophone will produce enough shock to have his presence recorded. The type of soil and background noise produced by travel on nearby roads and railroads determines the actual sensitivity of the system.

Many minerals are naturally radioactive. Some of these minerals are the ores of uranium or thorium and many geologists are employed in the exploration for these ores. Fortunately there are two common instruments, the *Geiger counter* and *scintillation counter* that detect radioactivity directly. In forensic work, radioactivity has been used in several ways: detecting radioactive minerals and use of radioactive powders and pastes that can later be detected with a counter showing that the person or object had contact with the paste or powder.

In a classic case in the late 1930's lead bars were stolen from the Palmer Physical Laboratory in Princeton, New Jersey. These bars were not ordinary lead bars, but contained radioactive cobalt. Assuming the thief disposed of the lead by selling them to a junkyard, investigators searched all the possible places in the area with a Geiger counter, and they discovered and recovered the lead.

Fluorescence

Many materials when exposed to ultraviolet light glow with a distinctive color. The color is normally different from the color of the material in normal white light. Indeed, some fluorescent materials are almost invisible in normal white light. Ultraviolet light has long been used to identify minerals that fluoresce and most museums have exhibits of spectacular fluorescent mineral displays.

Ultraviolet light, like all electromagnetic radiation, travels as a wave form. Electromagnetic wave lengths vary over a large spectrum from the longest radio waves of 20,000 meters to cosmic rays shorter than .0004 Angstrom units in length. The light we see ranges from violet, at approximately 3800 Angstrom units, to red at approximately 8000 Angstrom units. The ultraviolet range of wave lengths lies between approximately 1800 to 4000 Angstrom units. Commercially available ultraviolet lamps produce either "short radiation" in the ranges of from 1800 to 3000 Angstrom wave length or "long radiation" in the range of from 3000 to 4000 Angstrom unit wave length. Both these ranges are invisible to the human eye and the light that is commonly seen when these lamps are used is violet light that has not been removed. This visible light is useful because it tells us that the lamp is on and working.

When a fluorescent material is exposed to ultraviolet light the individual atoms in the material are excited and electrons that travel in small orbits around the nucleus of each atom jump to another orbit more distant from the nucleus. An electron in the outer orbit drops to replace the electron that moved. The movement of these electrons produces energy and the result is the generation of light that is visible to the human eye. Thus materials that fluoresce glow with visible light when excited with invisible light and may be seen and photographed. The color of the fluorescence, which will last only as long as the material is exposed to the ultraviolet light may be various shades of blue, brown, green, orange, gold, red, white, yellow, violet, or purple. The color depends on the material and in most cases is quite diagnostic. For example, the rock chips that are brought to the surface during the drilling of an oil well are examined under ultraviolet light because most oils fluoresce with distinctive colors. When rocks containing oil are penetrated, some of the oil sticks to the rock chips and gives a clue to the oil below.

In addition, it is possible to obtain pastes, powders and

sprays that fluoresce in a variety of colors such as shades of green, blue, and yellow. Recognition of the fluorescence on a suspect that has come in contact with objects sprayed or coated with one of these materials is generally quite easy and requires that the investigator be familiar with the fluorescent color being used. In cases of doubt, comparison with known samples of the fluorescent material can easily be made. Most of these materials respond when excited by both long- and short-wave fluorescent light. However, this should be checked to be sure that the light used is appropriate for the material. It appears that long-wave light is most commonly used with many of the commercially available materials. Short-wave-length ultraviolet light can be seriously damaging to the eyes and must be used with care. It is for this reason that the long-wave light is commonly used in identification kits.

Fluorescent paste is commonly placed on the tripping levers of fire alarm boxes as a means of identifying persons who sound false fire alarms. In one case a suspect was apprehended running away from the scene of a false fire alarm. His fingers were examined with the ultraviolet light and the skin showed a strong fluorescence. This was testified to during his trial. However, a second examination within two days of the apprehension revealed that the suspect wore a sport coat made of various synthetic fibers with fluorescent dyes. His hands were covered with perspiration and many of the loose fibers from the coat stuck to his hands. It was fibers and lint that were fluorescing. This was confirmed by removing the fibers from his hand and examining them under a microscope. Thus, the first identification was in error and the suspect's innocence was established. In order to be certain that the paste was not deliberately or accidentally removed in the two days between the original and second examination, a sample of the paste used was placed on several fingers and intense effort made to remove the material for several days. These efforts failed and the fluorescent material was still easily identifiable after several days. On occasion, finely ground distinctive minerals are mixed with a fluorescent paste or powder for use at a single location. Identification of the fluorescent material plus the minerals provides a truly individual identification. The person must have come in contact with the specific place where that specific paste had been placed.

Some rubber products such as tires are manufactured with oils that fluoresce under ultraviolet light. Thus it has been possible in some cases to recognize the imprint of an automobile tire on a clean concrete floor using ultraviolet light. Oil from the tire remains on the floor in much the same way that oils from a human finger remain on a surface to preserve a finger print. There has been some success in recording the intensity of ultraviolet light in the different ultraviolet wave lengths, thus characterizing the oils in certain tires. This offers the possibility of identifying the rubber products of different manufacturers from the impressions.

Water Currents

Geologists and oceanographers have long measured the velocity and direction of currents in the ocean, bays, and lakes. The geologic purpose of these measurements is to predict the movement of sediment, sand, and mud. In general, in an ocean, bay, or lake, the water will move along the bottom as a current. The direction and velocity may or may not be the same as the direction and velocity of a floating object which will be moved for the most part by the wind. In fact, currents with different velocities and directions commonly exist at different depths in the water mass.

Various methods are available for measuring the direction and velocity of these currents. For movement of currents along the bottom *drifter surveys* are normally made. Drifters are disks usually made of weighted plastic so that they are just heavy enough to rest on the bottom and move with the current. They are placed in the water at a known time and later recovered. By knowing the time it took for them to travel to the place of recovery it is possible to know how fast they drifted and thus the velocity of the current that moved them. Similar measurements can be made by placing a dye in the water and observing how fast the mass of water with the dye moves. Current meters of various types are available that record directly the velocity of water currents. The velocity of a floating object can be measured directly by recording the time it takes for it to move from one place to another in a given wind.

In general an unweighted human body will be denser than water for approximately six days after death and will thus act as a bottom drifter. After approximately six days a body will develop a lower density and float. The body thus becomes a surface drifter.

In some cases it has been possible, knowing the distribution of currents and their velocities, to reconstruct the location that a body was placed in the water or alternatively to predict the possible location of a body or other object if the time and point of entry are known.

The distribution and velocity of currents in San Francisco Bay have been studied for some time. Bottom drifter surveys have been made. Gangland style slayings in the San Francisco area have been followed by disposal of the bodies in the water of the bay near the Golden Gate. Bodies have been recovered along the shore at the southern end of the bay on both the east and west coasts. It has been possible to predict the time the body was dumped into the bay and the location of dumping, and anticipate the point where the bodies will surface. Knowing the surface wind-driven current, directions and velocities during a given time, it is possible to predict the place on land where the body will arrive. Such studies are not restricted to human bodies and with the appropriate information may be applied to any floating or bottom drifting object.

Aerial Photography

Aerial photographs are now used for a wide variety of purposes such as mapping and surveying, highway planning, geologic and forestry studies, archeology, crop damage, military operations, stockpile inventories, and many others. The American Society of Photogrammetry lists more than 100 different ways in which aerial photographs can serve a useful function. Many archeological discoveries have been made solely through the use of aerial photographs, some of which predate the Christian era. In the British Isles archeologic finds initially detected on aerial photographs date back to the Roman occupation. Aerial photographs have been used to help locate modern burial sites. The use of photography to locate burial grounds or other disturbed sites rests in general on the principle of a disturbed site having altered soil conditions, which in turn is colonized by plant spectra different from that of the adjacent undisturbed area. The surface of the soil in the disturbed area will have a different appearance than that of the adjacent undisturbed area. In the disturbed area the moisture regime will be altered as will the organic matter distribution, soil structure, and possibly other properties.

Many techniques used in aerial photography are as much an art as they are a science. Therefore, one cannot always foretell the best all-purpose film to use for photographing a particular sector. Further, the photo image may not be the same from day to day depending upon light moisture conditions and related factors. A certain image may be discernible on the ground on a certain day—but on another it may not. As the growing season progresses the image of the ground mosaic may change and in other situations the entire ground layer may be obliterated by the plant growth. In this connection selective films and filters are required in order to bring out certain features on the ground or in bodies of water.

For most purposes we are concerned with visible light images in the 3900–7600 Angstrom region of the light spectrum. Various films are used for photographing. *Panchromatic* film is suitable for most conventional work because it is sensitive to the same general region of the light spectrum as is the human eye. *Infrared* film is sensitive in the infrared region. Recordings on the infrared film are from infrared radiation, reflected or fluoresced, from an object. Pools of water absorb infrared light and register dark patterns. Recently cut vegetation can be distinguished from living healthy vegetation through the use of infrared film because the dead vegetation will not reflect as much radiation as will that which is living.

Color film is used to good advantage where there is need for rather detailed foliage analysis and water pollution information, as well as other studies. *Infrared color film,* also known as false color film, is useful in detecting recently killed vegetation, damaged plants, or artificial camouflage.

References

Avery, T. E. 1969. *Interpretation of aerial photographs,* 2nd ed. Minneapolis, Minn.: Burgess Publishing Co.

Colwell, R. N. 1973. Remote sensing as an aid to the management of earth resources. *American Scientist* 61(2):175–183.

Dobrin, M. B. 1960. *Introduction to geophysical prospecting,* 2nd ed. New York: McGraw-Hill Book Co.

Hurlbut, C. S. 1971. *Dana's manual of mineralogy,* 18th ed. New York: John Wiley & Sons, Inc.

Johnson, P. L. 1970. Remote sensing as an ecological tool in ecology of the subarctic regions. Proceedings of the Helsinki Symposium. No. 1: 169–187. Paris: UNESCO.

Moenssens, A. A., Moses, R. E., and Imbau, F. 1973. *Scientific evidence in criminal cases.* New York: Foundation Press.

9 Applying the Science

Soils and other earth materials have long been used in forensic matters. Expert testimony in this area is admissible in most jurisdictions and has made many contributions to justice. Moenssens et al. (1973) discuss the law with respect to scientific evidence. They cite the following criminal cases where information from soil or related material was admitted in evidence:

State v. Baldwin
47 N.J. 379, 221 A.2d 199 (1966) petition for certif. to App. Div. denied, 246 A.2d 459 (1968), *cert. denied* 385 U.S. 980.

Soil from crime scene was compared with soil from defendant's car.

State v. Spring
Supra n. 40.

Soil on boots was found to have evidential value.

State v. Atkinson
State v. Atkinson, 275 N.C. 288, 167 S.E.2d 241 (1969), remanded for resentencing, 183 S.E.2d 106 (1971).

Soil on shovel at defendant's home compared with soil from victim's burial scene.

176

Territory v. Young 32 Hawaii 628 (1933).	Soil on defendant's trousers compared with soil at rape scene. Defendant's alibi location produced samples that did not compare with soil on his trousers.
State v. Coolidge 109 N.H. 403, 260 A.2d 547 (1969) *rev'd* on other grounds 403 U.S. 443 (1971). Forty sets of particles were matched microscopically with regard to color, hue, and texture. Instrumentation found at least 27 sets to be indistinguishable in all tests.	Particles removed from victim's clothes compared to particles in suspect's automobile.
Aaron v. State 271 Ala. 70, 122 So.2d 360 (1960) *pet. for writ of error denied* 275 Ala. 377, 155 So.2d 334 (1963).	Dust from wall board broken during a rape compared with dust on the clothes of the defendant.
People v. Smith 142 Cal. App.2d 287, 298 P.2d 540 (1956).	Plaster dust implicated a burglary defendant.
State v. Washington 335 S.W.2d 23 (Mo. 1960).	Mortar particles on defendant's clothes compared with mortar found in the burglary access hole.

In other cases involving tools, dust on the tools was compared with material at the crime scene and this information was admitted in evidence, People v. Conley, 220 Cal.App.2d 296, 33 Cal. Rptr. 866 (1963): white plaster-like dust found on a hammer and a crowbar was similar to the dust at the crime scene; People v. Jenkins, 68 Ill.App.2d 215, 215 N.E.2d 302 (1966): red brick dust similar to that found at scene was removed from a sledge hammer.

The study of rocks, minerals, soils, and related material has many uses in forensic work. Because of the very large number of types and combinations their potential as physical evidence should be in many cases second only in value to truly individual objects such as fingerprints and some examples of tool mark and firearms comparisons. The use of these materials for both investigative and evidential purposes is limited by two factors:

1. They must be present in sufficient quantity for analysis.

2. The investigator must recognize their potential value and collect them for analysis.

Unlike many manufactured products, such as narcotics, or explosives or human products, such as blood or semen, where chemical identification alone may have evidential value, the earth materials require far more study and professional judgment. In addition, it is only seldom that a physical match can be made which uniquely shows that one sample was positively once part of another. This can sometimes be done with glass fragments or wood chips that were once part of a single piece.

During a strike several rocks were thrown through the windshield of a truck causing serious damage to property and persons. Several rock chips were collected from the suspect's vehicle. The rocks that inflicted the damage were also available for study and were shown to be limestone with abundant impressions of the fossils of ancient shellfish. Some of the rock chips found in the suspect's vehicle were fossils of the same type as those in the limestone. Indeed, fragments of fossils were found in the suspect's vehicle that matched perfectly the complex impressions of fossil shells in the limestone used as weapons. In this case we see a perfect physical "jig-saw" match of fossil and fossil impression on a rock. The two must have been once part of the same rock. Such evidence is seldom available and absolute individualization is only rarely possible.

In attempting to demonstrate comparison or lack of comparison, the forensic geologist, like other criminalists, commonly relies on finding particles of minerals, rocks, and related objects that are rare. For this reason, gross methods such as those that measure the density distribution, color, chemical composition, size distribution, may be of value in establishing comparison or lack of comparison but are seldom sufficient in themselves to make such a judgment. The study of the individual particles and their identification and amount when combined with these other methods are generally necessary. The generalist has an important role in forensic science, partially in recognizing the interrelations of the different kinds of physical evidence. However, for work in forensic geology and with many specialized studies, a person trained in the specialty is essential.

Thus, the possibility of a single standardized test for soils and related material as a basis for comparison is a desirable goal for research, but not something that is likely to be achieved in the immediate future. However, it is possible to outline a strategy for the study of these materials, recognizing that each type of material will be studied with the methods that will most likely lead to sound scientific judgment. In considering strategies, it is possible to divide the discussion into studies that serve as an aid to an investigation and those that seek to establish comparison or lack of comparison for use as evidence in a court of law. Needless to say, the distinction is not always clear-cut and preliminary studies made in an effort to assist an investigation may ultimately be used as evidence. The quality of the work should be of the same high order in all cases.

Studies to Assist an Investigation

The forensic geologist often receives samples, usually those associated with a crime or suspect, for study. The material is examined in the hope of identifying rocks, minerals, or other particles that would provide information useful in an investigation. The common quesion is, where could this material have come from? After studying the material and identifying the particles, the geologist can usually outline possible sources such as safe insulation or a certain geographic location. The quality of the answer depends on the unusualness of the material and the ability and experience of the scientist. In this type of study the stereobinocular microscope is normally the first instrument used. Examination with this instrument provides information on the types of material present. This may be followed by other methods, such as the scanning electron microscope, thin sections studied with the petrographic microscope or examination by X-ray diffraction.

Studies to Establish Comparison or Lack of Comparison

The purpose of these studies is to establish with a very high degree of probability that a given sample is similar to or dissimilar from another sample and that with an equally high degree of probability that the two samples came from, or could not have come from, the same small area. In challenging this type of evidence two questions are normally asked:

1. If you were to sample some distance away would you find similar material? That is, is the material with the same properties common over a wide area? We need much more information and research on the rate at which properties of soils and related material actually change over short distances. However, this question is normally answered by study of samples collected away from the immediate scene and a professional choice of properties that are known to change rapidly.

2. Is there another place on the earth where an exactly similar sample *might* exist? In most cases, a question of this type can only be answered "Yes." Soils and related material are not generally individual type items such as fingerprints and evidence based on their study can only be stated in terms of samples being similar or dissimilar; comparable or not comparable. Soil samples approach individuality when several methods are used and "unusual" minerals or combinations of minerals are found.

The scientist who is experienced with these problems will have developed a set of procedures appropriate to the types of earth materials normally encountered. However, the following sequence of procedures is suggested as a working model (Fig. 9-1):

The sample is first compared for color, using natural light. The individual size grades may also be compared for color. The whole sample is studied under the stereobinocular microscope and unusual particles that may have value to other specialists, such as hair, fiber, paint, glass, plastics, etc., are removed. The sample is then size sorted to produce a sample having the same sizes of particles. The smallest size grades are saved for possible study by X-ray diffraction, scanning electron microscope, chemical or other instrumental analysis.

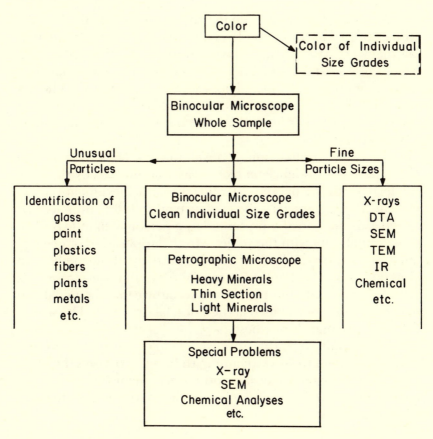

Figure 9-1   Flow diagram for study of earth materials for forensic purposes.

The coarser material is studied under the stereobinocular microscope, and the kinds of particles are identified and counted. At this stage it may be desirable to make further studies with the petrographic microscope of thin sections or grain mounts. Alternatively, other visual, chemical or physical methods, such as the scanning electron microscope, X-ray diffraction, etc., may be used. Each stage in the examination suggests the appropriate next step until the scientist is satisfied that the samples compare or do not compare, and is prepared to defend his judgment.

Anyone who has worked in this area is regretfully familiar with examples of testimony given in cases involving earth materials that were based on inadequate study. In the authors' experience, these examples of poor evidence have come from both defense and prosecution and both sides in civil matters. There is no excuse for the submission of evidence in a court of law that relies on methods or ideas that were outmoded and inadequate fifty years ago.

By way of comparison, it is well to consider a hypothetical trial where the evidence on blood was accumulated by the most modern methods backed by remarkable achievements in research. At this same trial the evidence on soils was prepared by casual examination and presented by a person with little professional familiarity with the subject. In the application of geology and soil science to oil finding today, we use few of the methods in general use in the 1920's. Successful oil finders recognize this and all forensic laboratories should recognize that their goal is to match the work performed at the finest laboratories. The search for justice demands our best.

It is equally true that forensic geology can only serve the cause of justice if the investigator in the case recognizes the value of soils and related materials and collects them for study. The challenge for the future is the production of the best evidence to serve justice.

Glossary *

ACIDIC. Applied loosely to any igneous rock composed predominantly of light-colored minerals having a low specific gravity and greater than 65 percent silica.

ACID SOIL. A soil with a preponderance of hydrogen ions, and probably of aluminum, in proportion to hydroxyl ions. For most practical purposes a soil with a pH value 6.6 or less.

ACRE. A unit of land area used in the U.S. and England, equal to 43,560 square feet (approximately 208 feet^2), 4840 square yards, 160 square rods, 1/640 square miles.

AIR-DRY. The state of dryness (of a soil) at equilibrium with the moisture content in the surrounding atmosphere.

ALABASTER. A firm, very fine-grained, and massive or compact variety of gypsum, usually snow-white and translucent but sometimes delicately shaded or tinted.

ALBITE. A colorless or milky-white triclinic mineral of the feldspar group: $NaAlSi_3O_8$. It is a variety of plagioclase with composition ranging from $Ab_{100}An_0$ to $Ab_{90}An_{10}$; it is also an alkali feldspar.

ALKALI FELDSPAR. A group of feldspars composed of mixtures, or mixed crystals, of potassium feldspar and sodium feldspar.

ALKALI SOIL. A soil with a high degree of alkalinity or with a high exchangeable sodium content that contains sufficient alkali to interfere with the growth of most crop plants.

ALLUVIAL. Pertaining to or composed of alluvium, or deposited by a stream or running water.

AMBER. A very hard, brittle, usually yellowish to brownish, translucent or transparent fossil resin derived from coniferous trees, that frequently encloses insects and other organisms.

* The following terms have been modified from *Glossary of Geology*, edited by Gary, McAfee and Wolf, published by the American Geological Institute, 857 pp., 1972, and Glossary of Soil Science Terms, *Soil Science, Soc. Amer. Proc.* 29:330–351, 1965. It is suggested that the reader consult these volumes for additional information and other terms.

AMETHYST. A transparent to translucent and purple, purple-red, reddish-purple, bluish-violet, or pale-violet variety of crystalline quartz.

AMORPHOUS. Said of a mineral or other substance that lacks crystalline structure.

AMPHIBOLE. A group of dark, rock-forming, ferromagnesian silicate minerals closely related in crystal form and composition and having the general formula: $A_{2-3}B_5(Si, Al)_8O_{22}(OH)_2$, where $A = Mg$, Fe^{2+}, Ca, or Na, and $B = Mg$, Fe^{2+}, Fe^{3+}, or Al.

AMYGDULE. A gas cavity or vesicle in an igneous rock which is filled with such secondary minerals as zeolite, calcite, quartz or chalcedony.

ANDALUSITE. A brown, yellow, green, red, or gray orthorhombic mineral: Al_2SiO_5.

ANDESINE. A mineral of the plagioclase feldspar group with composition ranging from $Ab_{70}An_{30}$ to $Ab_{50}An_{50}$. It occurs as a primary constituent of intermediate igneous rocks.

ANDESITE. A dark-colored, fine-grained extrusive rock that, when porphyritic, contains phenocrysts composed primarily of zoned acid plagioclase in the range of An_{35} to An_{70} and one or more of the magic minerals (e.g., biotite, hornblende, pyroxene).

ANGLE OF REPOSE. The maximum angle of slope, measured from a horizontal plane, at which loose, cohesionless material will come to rest on a pile of similar material.

ANHYDRITE. A mineral consisting of an anhydrous calcium sulfate: $CaSO_4$.

ANISOTROPIC. Said of a medium whose physical properties vary in different directions.

ANORTHITE. A white grayish, or reddish triclinic mineral of the plagioclase feldspar group: $CaAl_2Si_2O_8$.

ANORTHOSITE. A group of essentially monomineralic plutonic igneous rocks composed almost entirely of plagioclase feldspar.

ANTHRACITE. Coal of the highest metamorphic rank, in which fixed-carbon content is between 92 percent and 98 percent.

APATITE. A group of variously colored hexagonal minerals consisting of calcium phosphate together with fluorine, chlorine, hydroxyl, or carbonate in varying amounts and having the general formula: $Ca_5(PO_4, CO_3)_3(F, OH, Cl)$.

APHANITIC. Said of the texture of an igneous rock in which the crystalline components are not distinguishable by the unaided eye.

ARAGONITE. A white, yellowish, or gray orthorhombic mineral: $CaCO_3$.

ARENACEOUS. Said of a sediment or sedimentary rock consisting wholly or in part of sand-size fragments.

ARGILLACEOUS. Pertaining to, largely composed of, or containing clay-size particles or clay minerals.

ARGILLITE. A compact rock, derived either from mudstone or shale, that has undergone a somewhat high degree of induration.

ARKOSE. A feldspar-rich, typically coarse-grained sandstone, commonly pink or reddish to pale gray or buff, composed of angular to subangular grains that may be either poorly or moderately well-sorted, usually derived from the rapid disintegration of granite or granitic rocks.

ASBESTOS. A commercial term applied to a group of highly fibrous silicate minerals that readily separate into long, thin, strong fibers of sufficient flexibility to be woven.

AUGITE. A common mineral of the clinopyroxene group. It may contain titanium and ferric iron. Augite is usually black, greenish black, or dark green.

AVAILABLE WATER. The portion of water in a soil that can be readily absorbed by plant roots.

BASALT. A dark to medium-dark colored, commonly extrusive mafic igneous rock composed chiefly of calcic plagioclase and clinopyroxene in a glassy or fine-grained groundmass; the extrusive equivalent of gabbro.

BASIC. Said of an igneous rock having a relatively low silica content, sometimes delimited arbitrarily as less than 54 percent.

BAUXITE. An off-white, grayish, brown, yellow, or reddish-brown rock composed of a mixture of various amorphous or crystalline hydrous aluminum oxides and aluminum hydroxides.

BENCH MARK. A relatively permanent metal tablet or other mark firmly embedded in a fixed and enduring natural or artificial object, indicating a precisely determined elevation above or below a standard datum, usually sea level.

BENTONITE. A soft, plastic, porous, light-colored rock consisting largely of colloidal silica and composed essentially of clay minerals in the form of extremely minute crystals, and produced by devitrification and accompanying chemical alteration of a glassy igneous material.

BERYL. A mineral: $Be_3Al_2Si_6O_{18}$. It usually occurs in green or bluish-green, sometimes yellow or pink, or rarely white, hexagonal prisms.

BIOTITE. A dark-colored mineral of the mica group: $K(MgFe)_3AlSi_3O_{10}(OH)$.

BLACK SAND. An alluvial or beach sand consisting predominantly of grains of heavy, dark minerals or rocks.

BOG SOIL. A great soil group of the intrazonal order and hydromorphic suborder; includes muck and peat.

BOG IRON ORE. A general term for a soft, spongy, and porous deposit of impure hydrous iron oxides formed in bogs, marches, swamps, peat mosses, and shallow lakes by precipitation from iron-bearing waters.

BORAX. A white, yellowish, blue, green or gray mineral: $Na_2B_4O_7 \cdot 10H_2O$.

BRACHIOPOD. Any solitary marine invertebrate belonging to the phylum *Brachiopoda*. Fossil shells are common in Paleozoic sedimentary rocks.

BRAIDED STREAM. A stream that divides into or follows an interlacing or tangled network of several small, branching, and reuniting shallow channels separated from each other by branch islands or channel bars, resembling in plan the strands of a complex braid.

BRECCIA. A coarse-grained clastic rock composed of large, angular, and broken rock fragments that are cemented together in a finer-grained matrix.

BRUNTON COMPASS. A small, compact pocket surveying instrument that consists of an ordinary compass, folding open sights, a mirror, and a rectangular spirit-level clinometer and that can be used in the hand or upon a staff or light rod for reading horizontal and vertical angles, for leveling, and for reading the magnetic bearing of a line.

BRYOZOAN. Any invertebrate belonging to the phylum *Bryozoa* and characterized chiefly by colonial growth. Fossils are common in many Postcambrian sedimentary rocks.

CALCITE. A common rock-forming mineral: $CaCo_3$.

CARBONATE ROCK. A rock consisting chiefly of carbonate minerals, such as limestone, dolomite, or carbonatite.

CARBON NITROGEN RATIO. The ratio of the weight of organic carbon to the weight of total nitrogen in a soil or in organic material.

CARBON-14 DATING. A method of determining an age in years by measuring the concentration of carbon-14 remaining in an organic material, usually formerly living matter.

CARNELIAN. A translucent blood-red, flesh-red, reddish-white, orange-red, reddish-yellow, or brownish-red variety of chalcedony.

CASSITERITE. A brown or black tetragonal mineral: SnO_2. It is the principal ore of tin.

CAST. A sedimentary structure representing the infilling of an original mark or depression made on top of a soft bed. It is also a secondary rock or mineral material that fills a natural mold.

CATENA. A sequence of soils of about the same age, derived from similar parent material, and occurring under similar climatic conditions, but having different characteristics due to variation in relief and in drainage.

CATION EXCHANGE. The interchange between a cation in solution and another cation of the surface of any surface-active material such as clay colloid or organic colloid.

CATION-EXCHANGE-CAPACITY. The sum total of exchangeable cations that a soil can absorb.

CHALCEDONY. A cryptocrystalline variety of quartz.

CHALK. A soft, pure, earthy, fine-textured, usually white to light gray or buff limestone of marine origin, consisting almost wholly of calcite, formed mainly by shallow-water accumulation of calcareous tests of floating micro-organisms and of comminuted remains of calcareous algae set in a structureless matrix of very finely crystalline calcite.

CHERT. A hard, extremely dense or compact, dull to semivitreous, cryptocrystalline sedimentary rock, consisting dominantly of cryptocrystalline silica.

CHLORITE. A group of platy, monoclinic, usually greenish minerals of general formula: $(MgFe^{2+}, Fe^{3+})_6AlSi_3O_{10}(OH)_8$. It is characterized by prominent ferrous iron and by the absence of calcium and alkalies; chromium and manganese may also be present. Chlorites are associated with and resemble the micas.

CHROMITE. A brownish to iron-black mineral of the spinel group: $(Fe, Mg)(Cr, Al)_2O_4$. It occurs in octahedral crystals as a primary accessory mineral in basic and ultrabasic igneous rocks; it also occurs massive, and it forms detrital deposits.

CHRYSOCOLLA. A blue, blue-green, or emerald-green mineral: $(Cu_2H_2(Si_2O_5)(OH)_4$. It is usually cryptocrystalline or amorphous, and it occurs as incrustations and thin seams in the zone of weathering of copper ores.

CLAY MINERAL. One of a complex and loosely defined group of finely crystalline, metacolloidal, or amorphous hydrous silicates essentially of aluminum.

COAL. A readily combustible rock containing more than 50 percent by weight and more than 70 percent by volume of carbonaceous material including inherent moisture, formed from compaction and induration of variously altered plant remains similar to those in peat. Differences in the kinds of plant materials in degree of metamorphism and in the range of impurity are characteristics of coal and used in classification.

COLLUVIUM. A deposit of rock fragments and soil material accumulated at the base of steep slopes as a result of gravitational action.

CONCRETION. A hard, compact, rounded, normally subspherical mass or aggregate of mineral matter generally formed by orderly and localized precipitation from aqueous solution.

CONGLOMERATE. A coarse-grained, clastic sedimentary rock composed of rounded to subangular fragments larger than 2 mm in diameter set in a fine-grained matrix of sand, silt, or any of the common natural cementing materials.

CONSOLIDATION. Any process whereby loosely aggregated, soft, or liquid earth materials become firm and coherent rock.

CONTACT. A plane or irregular surface between two different types or ages of rocks.

COPROLITE. The fossilized excrement of vertebrates such as fishes, reptiles and mammals.

COQUINA. A detrital limestone composed wholly or chiefly of mechanically sorted fossil debris that experienced abrasion and transport before reaching the depositional site and that is weakly to moderately cemented but not completely compacted and indurated.

CORAL. A general name for any of a large group of bottom-dwelling, sessile, marine invertebrate organisms that belong to the class *Anthozoa.*

CREEP. The slow, gradual, more or less continuous, nonrecoverable deformation sustained by ice, soil, and rock materials under gravitational body stresses.

CRINOID. Any pelmatozoan echinoderm belonging to the class *Crinoidea.* These fossil "sea lilies" are common in many Postcambrian sedimentary rocks.

CROSS-BEDDING. An internal arrangement of the layers in a stratified rock, characterized by minor beds or laminae inclined more or less regularly in straight sloping lines or concave forms at various angles.

and during a specified period of time, by evaporation from the soil surface and by transpiration from plants.

EXTRUSIVE. Said of igneous rock that has been ejected onto the surface of the earth. They include lava flows and detrital material such as volcanic ash.

FAULT. A surface or zone of rock fracture along which there has been displacement, from a few centimeters to a few kilometers in scale.

FELDSPAR. A group of abundant rock-forming minerals of general formula: $MAl(Al, Si)_3O_8$ where M = K, Na, Ca, Ba, Rb, Sr, and Fe. Feldspars are the most widespread of any mineral group and constitute 60 percent of the earth's crust.

FELSITE. A light-colored, fine-grained extrusive or hypabyssal rock with or without phenocrysts and composed chiefly of quartz and feldspar.

FISSILITY. A general term for the property possessed by some rocks of splitting easily into thin sheets or layers along closely spaced, roughly planar, and approximately parallel surfaces.

FLAGSTONE. A hard, evenly and thin-bedded, usually micaceous and fine-grained sandstone that splits readily and uniformly along bedding planes or joints into large, thin, flat slabs suitable for making pavements or covering the side of a house.

FIELD CAPACITY. The percentage of water remaining in a soil 2 or 3 days after having been saturated and after free drainage has practically ceased.

FLINT. A term that has been considered as a mineral name for a massive, very hard, somewhat impure variety of chalcedony.

FLUORITE. A transparent to translucent mineral: CaF_2.

FOSSIL. Any remains, trace, or imprint of a plant or animal that has been preserved, by natural processes, in the earth's crust since some past geologic time.

FULLER'S EARTH. A very fine-grained, naturally occurring earthy substance possessing a high adsorptive capacity, consisting largely of hydrated aluminum silicates.

GABBRO. A group of dark-colored, basic intrusive igneous rocks composed principally of basic plagioclase and clino-pyroxene, with or without olivine and orthopyroxene.

GALENA. A bluish-gray to lead-gray mineral: PbS.

GARNET. A group of minerals of formula: $A_3B_2(SiO_4)_3$. Where A = Ca, Mg, Fe^{2+} and Mn^{2+}, and B = Al, Fe^{3+}, Mn^{3+} and Cr.

GASTROPOD. Any mollusk belonging to the class *Gastropoda*, characterized by a distinct head with eyes and tentacles and, in most, by a
single calcareous shell that is closed at the apex, sometimes spiral-
led, not chambered, and generally asymmetrical.

GEMSTONE. Any mineral, rock, or other natural material that, when cut
and polished, has the necessary beauty and durability or hardness
for use as a personal adornment or other ornament.

GEODE. A hollow or partly hollow and globular or subspherical body,
from 2.5 cm to 30 cm or more in diameter, found in certain
limestone beds.

GEOPHYSICAL SURVEY. The use of one or more geophysical techniques
in geophysical exploration, such as earth currents, electrical,
infra-red, heat flow, magnetic, radioactivity and seismic.

GEYSER. A type of hot spring that intermittently erupts jets of hot water
and steam, the result of ground water coming into contact with
rock or steam hot enough to create steam under conditions preventing free circulation.

GLACIER. A large mass of ice formed, at least in part, on land by the
compaction and recrystallization of snow.

GLAUCONITE. A dull green, amorphous, and earthy or granular mineral of the mica group: $(K, Na) (Al, Fe^{3+}, Mg)_2(AlSi)_4O_{10}(OH)_2$.
Glauconite occurs abundantly in greensand, and seems to be forming in the marine environment at the present time.

GLEY SOIL. Soil developed under conditions of poor drainage resulting
in reduction of iron and other elements and in gray colors and
mottles.

GNEISS. A foliated rock formed by regional metamorphism in which
bands or lenticles of granular minerals alternate with bands and
lenticles in which minerals having flaky or elongate prismatic
habits predominate.

GOETHITE. A yellowish, reddish, or brownish-black iron-bearing mineral, goethite is the most common constituent of many forms of
natural rust.

GRANITE. A coarse-grained plutonic rock in which quartz constitutes 10
to 50 percent of the felsic components.

GRANODIORITE. A group of coarse-grained plutonic rocks intermediate
in composition between quartz diorite and quartz monzonite, containing quartz, plagioclase, and potassium feldspar, with biotite,
hornblende, or, more rarely, pyroxene, as the mafic components.

GRAPHITE. A hexagonal mineral, representing a naturally occurring crystalline form of carbon dimorphous with diamond. It is

opaque, lustrous, very soft, greasy to the touch, and iron black to steel gray in color; it occurs as crystals or flakes, scales, laminae, or grains.

GREENSAND MARL. A marl containing sand-size grains of glauconite.

GROUND WATER. That part of the subsurface water that is the zone of saturation, including underground streams.

GUANO. A phosphate deposit formed by the leaching of bird excrement accumulated in arid regions.

GUMBO. A term used locally in the U.S. for a fine-grained clay soil that becomes sticky, impervious, and plastic when wet.

GYPSUM. A widely distributed mineral consisting of hydrous calcium sulfate: $CaSO_4 \cdot 2H_2O$. It is the commonest sulfate mineral and is frequently associated with halite and anhydrite in evaporites.

HALITE. A mineral: NaCl. It is native salt, occurring in massive granular, compact or cubic-crystalline forms.

HALOPHYTIC VEGETATION. Salt-loving or salt tolerant vegetation.

HARDPAN. A general term for a relatively hard, impervious, and often clayey layer of soil lying at or just below the surface, produced as a result of cementation of soil particles by precipitation of relatively insoluble materials such as silica, iron oxide, calcium carbonate, and organic matter, offering exceptionally great resistance to digging or drilling, and permanently hampering root penetration and downward movement of water.

HEAVY SOIL. A soil with a high content of the fine separates, particularly clay.

HEXAGONAL SYSTEM. One of the six crystal systems. See Figure 3-3.

HORNBLENDE. The commonest mineral of the amphibole group: $Ca_2Na(Mg, Fe^{2+})_4(Al, Fe^{3+}, Ti)(Al,Si_8O_{22})(O,OH)_2$. Commonly black, dark green or brown, and occurs in distinct monoclinic crystals.

HUMIC ACID. A mixture of variable or indefinite composition of dark-colored organic substances, precipitated upon acidification of a dilute-alkali extract from soil.

HUMUS. That more or less stable fraction of the soil organic matter remaining after the major portion of added plant and animal residues have decomposed.

HYDROTHERMAL. Of or pertaining to heated water, to the action of heated water, or to the products of the action of heated water, such as a mineral deposit precipitated from a hot aqueous solution.

ICE AGE. A loosely used synonym of glacial epoch, or the time of extensive glacial activity; specifically the Ice Age, or the latest of the glacial epochs known as the Pleistocene.

IGNEOUS. Said of a rock or mineral that solidified from molten or partly molten material called a magma.

ILLITE. A general name for a group of three-layer, mica-like, and gray, light-green, or yellowish brown clay minerals that are widely distributed in argillaceous sediments that are intermediate in composition and structure between muscovite and montmorillonite.

ILLUVIATION. The process of deposition of soil material removed from one horizon to another in the soil; usually from an upper to a lower horizon in the soil profile.

ILMENITE. An iron-black, opaque rhombohedral mineral: $FeTiO_3$. Occurs as a common accessory mineral in basic igneous rocks.

IMPEDED DRAINAGE. A condition which hinders the movement of water through soils under the influence of gravity.

IMPERVIOUS. Resistant to penetration by fluids or by roots.

INFILTRATION RATE. A soil characteristic determining or describing the maximum rate at which water can enter the soil under specified conditions, including the presence of an excess of water.

INSOLUBLE RESIDUE. The material remaining after a more soluble part of a specimen has been dissolved in hydrochloric acid or acetic acid.

ION EXCHANGE. The reversible replacement of certain ions by others, without loss of crystal structure.

ISINGLASS. A synonym of mica.

ISOBATH. In oceanography, a line on a map or chart that connects points of equal water depth.

ISOMETRIC SYSTEM. One of the six crystal systems. See Figure 3-3.

ISOPACH. A line drawn on a map through points of equal thickness of a designated stratigraphic unit or group of stratigraphic units.

ISOTROPIC. Said of a medium whose properties are the same in all directions.

JADE. A hard, extremely tough, compact gemstone consisting of either the pyroxene mineral jadeite or the amphibole mineral nephrite, and having an unevenly distributed color ranging from dark or deep green to dull or greenish white.

JASPER. A dense, cryptocrystalline, opaque variety of chert associated with iron ores and containing iron oxides that give the rock various colors.

JOINT. A surface of actual or potential fracture or parting in a rock, without displacement.

KAOLIN. A group of clay minerals characterized by a two-layer crystal lattice.

KARST. A type of topography that is formed over limestone, dolomite, or gypsum by dissolving or solution, and that is characterized by closed depressions or sinkholes, caves and underground drainage.

KYANITE. A blue or light-green triclinic mineral: Al_2SiO_5.

LABRADORITE. A dark mineral of the plagioclase feldspar group. It commonly shows a rich, beautiful play of vivid colors and is therefore much used for ornamental purposes.

LACUSTRINE. Pertaining to, produced by, or formed in a lake or lakes.

LAMINA. The thinnest or smallest, recognizable unit layer of original deposition in a sediment or sedimentary rock, differing from other layers in color, composition or particle size.

LAVA. A general term for molten extrusive; also for the rock that is solidified from it.

LIMESTONE. A sedimentary rock consisting chiefly of calcium carbonate, primarily in the form of the mineral calcite. A rock containing 95 percent calcite and less than 5 percent dolomite.

LIMONITE. A general field term for a group of brown, amorphous, naturally occurring hydrous iron oxides.

LOESS. A widespread, homogeneous, commonly nonstratified, porous, friable, unconsolidated but slightly coherent fine-grained wind deposit. It is believed to be wind blown dust of Pleistocene age.

LUSTER. The reflection of light from the surface of a mineral described by its quality and intensity.

MACROCRYSTALLINE. Said of the texture of a rock consisting of or having crystals that are large enough to be distinctly visible to the unaided eye or with a simple hand lens.

MACROFOSSIL. A fossil large enough to be studied without the aid of a microscope.

MAGMA. Naturally occurring molten rock material, generated within the Earth.

MALACHITE. A bright-green monoclinic mineral: $Cu_2CO_3(OH)_2$. It is an ore of copper.

MANTLE ROCK. A synonym of regolith.

MARBLE. A metamorphic rock consisting predominantly of fine to coarse-grained recrystallized calcite and/or dolomite.

MARCASITE. A common, very light brownish-yellow or grayish orthorhombic mineral: FeS_2.

MARL. An old term loosely applied to a variety of materials most of which occur as soft, loose, earthy and semi-friable or crumbling unconsolidated deposits consisting chiefly of an intimate mixture of clay and calcium in varying proportions, formed under either marine or especially freshwater conditions.

MEANDER. One of a series of somewhat regular, sharp, freely developing, and sinuous curves, bends, loops, turns, or windings in the course of a stream.

MEAN HIGH WATER. The average height of all the higher high waters recorded at a given place over a nineteen-year period or a computed equivalent period.

MEAN LOW WATER. The average height of all the low waters recorded a a given place over a nineteen-year period or a computed equivalent period.

MEAN SEA LEVEL. The average height of the surface of the sea for all stages of the tide over a nineteen-year period, usually determined from hourly height observations on an open coast or in adjacent waters having free access to the sea.

MECHANICAL ANALYSIS. Determination of the particle-size distribution of a soil, sediment, or rock by screening, sieving, or other means of mechanical separation.

METAMORPHIC ROCK. Any rock derived from pre-existing rocks by mineralogical, chemical and structural changes, essentially in the solid state, in response to marked changes in temperature, pressure, shearing stress, and chemical environment at depth in the Earth's crust.

MICA. A group of silicate minerals with one perfect cleavage. See BIOTITE and MUSCOVITE.

MICROCLINE. A clear, white to light-gray, pale-yellow, brick-red or green mineral of the alkali feldspar group.

MICROCRYSTALLINE. Said of the texture of a rock consisting of or having crystals that are small enough to be visible only under the microscope.

MICRONUTRIENT. A chemical element necessary in only extremely small amounts for the growth of plants.

MILITARY GEOLOGY. The application of the earth sciences, especially soil science and climatology, to military concerns, such as water resources, etc.

MOLD. An impression made in the surrounding earth or rock material by the exterior or interior of a fossil shell or other organic structure.

MOHS' SCALE. A standard of ten minerals by which the hardness of a mineral may be rated.

MONOCHROMATOR. An instrument for selecting a narrow portion of a light spectrum.

MONOCLINIC. One of the six crystal systems. See Figure 3-3.

MONTMORILLONITE. A group of expanding-lattice clay minerals of general formula: $R_{0.33}Al_2Si_4O_{10}(OH)_2nH_2O$, where R includes one or more of the cations Na^+, K^+, Mg^{2+}, Ca^{2+} and possibly others.

MOONSTONE. A semitransparent to translucent alkali feldspar that exhibits a bluish to milky-white, pearly or opaline luster.

MOR. A type of forest humus in which the H layer is present and in which there is practically no mixing of surface organic matter with mineral soil.

MORAINE. A mound, ridge, or other distinct accumulation of unsorted, unstratified glacial drift, predominantly till, deposited chiefly by direct action of glacier ice in a variety of topographic landforms controlled by the surface on which the drift lies.

MOTTLE. A spot, blotch, or patch of color or shade of color, occurring on the surface of a sediment or soil.

MUD. A slimy and sticky or slippery mixture of water and finely divided particles or solid or earthy material, with a consistency varying from semifluid to that of a soft and plastic sediment.

MULL. A type of forest humus in which the F layer may or may not be present and in which there is no H layer.

MUNSELL COLOR SYSTEM. A system of color classification that is applied in geology to the colors of rocks and soils.

MUSCOVITE. A light-colored mineral of the mica group: $KAl_2(AlSi_3)O_{10}(OH)_2$.

NEPHELINE SYENITE. A plutonic rock composed essentially of alkali feldspar and nepheline.

NODULE. A small, hard, and irregular, rounded or tuberous body of a mineral or mineral aggregate, normally having a warty or knobby surface and no internal structure, and usually exhibiting a contrasting composition from and a greater hardness than the enclosing sediment or rock matrix in which it is embedded.

OBSIDIAN. A black or dark-colored volcanic glass, usually of rhyolite composition characterized by conchoidal fracture.

OIL SHALE. A kerogen-bearing, finely laminated brown or black shale that will yield liquid or gaseous hydrocarbons on distillation.

OLIGOTROPHIC LAKE. A lake that is characterized by a deficiency in plant nutrients and usually by abundant dissolved oxygen; its bottom deposits have relatively small amounts of slowly decaying organic matter and its water is often deep.

OLIVINE. An olive-green, grayish-green, or brown orthorhombic mineral: $(Mg, Fe)_2SiO_4$.

ONYX. A variety of chalcedony that is like banded agate in consisting of alternating bands of different colors but unlike it in that the bands are always straight and parallel.

OOLITH. One of the small, round accretionary bodies in a sedimentary rock, resembling the roe of fish.

OPAL. A mineral: $SiO_2 \cdot nH_2O$. It is an amorphous form of silica containing varying proportion of water and occurring in nearly all colors.

ORTHOCLASE. A colorless, white, cream-yellow, flesh-reddish or grayish mineral of the alkali feldspar group: $KAlSi_3O_8$.

ORTHORHOMBIC SYSTEM. One of six crystal systems. See Figure 3-3.

OSTRACODE. Any aquatic crustacean belonging to the subclass Ostracoda, characterized by a bivalve, generally calcified carapace with a hinge along the dorsal margin.

OUTWASH. Stratified detritus removed or "washed out" from a glacier by meltwater streams and deposited in front of or beyond the terminal moraine or the margin of an active glacier.

OVERGROWTH. Secondary material deposited in optical and crystallographic continuity around a crystal grain of the same composition.

PALYNOLOGY. A branch of science concerned with the study of pollen of seed plants and spores of other embryophytic plants, whether living or fossil, including their dispersal and applications in stratigraphy and paleoecology.

PARENT MATERIAL. The unconsolidated and more or less chemically weathered mineral or organic matter from which the solum of soils is developed by pedogenic processes.

PARTICLE SIZE. The effective diameter of a particle measured by sedimentation, sieving, or micrometric methods.

PEAT. Unconsolidated soil material consisting largely of undecomposed, or slightly decomposed, organic matter accumulated under conditions of excessive moisture.

PEGMATITE. An exceptionally coarse-grained igneous rock, with interlocking crystals, usually found as irregular dikes, lenses or veins.

PERCHED GROUND WATER. Unconfined ground water separated from an underlying main body of ground water by an unsaturated zone.

PERIDOTITE. A general term for a coarse-grained plutonic rock composed chiefly of olivine with or without other mafic minerals and containing little or no feldspars.

PETROLOGY. The branch of geology dealing with the origin, occurrence, structure, and history of rocks, especially igneous or metamorphic rocks.

PHENOCRYST. A term widely used for a relatively large, conspicuous crystal in a porphyritic rock.

PHI GRADE SCALE. A logarithmic transformation of the Wentworth grade scale in which the negative logarithm to the base 2 of the particle diameter is substituted for the diameter value.

pH SOIL. The negative logarithm of the hydrogen-ion activity of a soil; the degree of acidity or alkalinity of a soil.

PLACER. A surficial mineral deposit formed by mechanical concentration of mineral particles from weathered debris.

PLAGIOCLASE. A group of triclinic feldspars of general formula: $(Na, Ca)Al(Si, Al)Si_2O_8$. One of the commonest rock-forming minerals; have characteristic twinning and often display zoning. The composition is usually described by stating the percent albite (ab) and the percent andorthite (an) in the sample, for example, ab_{40}, an_{60}.

PLANKTON. Aquatic organisms that drift or swim weakly.

PLEOCHROISM. The ability or property of an anisotropic crystal to absorb differentially various wavelengths of transmitted light in various crystallographic directions, and thus to show different colors in different directions.

POINT COUNTER ANALYSIS. A statistical method involving the estimation of the frequency of occurrence of an object such as a fossil or mineral species, in a sample determined by counting the number of times that object occurs at specified intervals throughout the sample.

PORPHYRY. An igneous rock of any composition that contains conspicuous phenocrysts in a fine-grained groundmass.

PRESSURE SOLUTION. Solution occurring preferentially at the contact surfaces of grains where the external pressure exceeds the hydraulic pressure of the interstitial fluid.

PROSPECTOR. An individual engaged in prospecting for valuable mineral deposits.

PUDDINGSTONE. A popular name applied chiefly in Great Britain to a conglomerate consisting of well-rounded pebbles whose colors are in such marked contrast with the abundant fine-grained matrix or cement that in section the rock suggests an old-fashioned pudding containing plums or raisins.

PUMICE. A light-colored, vesicular, glassy rock commonly having the composition of a rhyolite. It is often sufficiently buoyant to float on water and is economically useful as a light-weight aggregate and as an abrasive.

PYRITE. A common, pale-bronze or brass-yellow, isometric mineral: FeS_2.

PYROCLASTIC ROCK. A rock that is composed of materials fragmented by volcanic explosion; characterized by a lack of sorting.

PYROPHYLLITE. A white, greenish, gray, or brown mineral: $AlSi_2O_5$ (OH).

PYROXENE. A group of dark, rock-forming silicate minerals closely related in crystal form and composition and having the formula: $ABSi_2O_6$, where A = Ca, Na, Mg, or Fe^{2+} and B = Mg, Fe^{3+}, or Al with silicon sometimes replaced partly by aluminum.

QUARTZ. Crystalline silica, an important rock-forming mineral: SiO_2. Next to feldspar, the commonest mineral.

QUARTZITE. (Metamorphic definition.) A granoblastic metamorphic rock consisting mainly of quartz and formed by recrystallization of sandstone or chert by either regional or thermal metamorphism.

QUARTZITE. (Sedimentary definition.) A very hard but unmetamorphosed sandstone consisting chiefly of quartz grains that have been so completely and solidly cemented with secondary silica that the rock breaks across or through the individual grains rather than around them.

RADIOLARIAN OOZE. An ooze whose skeletal remains consist of the opaline silica tests of radiolarians.

RADIOMETRIC DATING. Calculating an age in years for geologic materials by measuring the presence of a short-life radioactive element or by measuring the presence of a long-life radioactive element plus its decay product.

REACTION, SOIL. The degree of acidity or alkalinity of a soil usually expressed as a pH value.

RED BEDS. Sedimentary strata deposited in a continental environment, composed largely of sandstone, siltstone, and shale with locally thin units of conglomerate, limestone, or marl, and are predominantly red in color due to the presence of ferric oxide usually coating individual grains.

RED TIDE. A type of water bloom that is caused by dinoflagellates.

REFRACTOMETER. An apparatus for measuring the indices of refraction of a substance, either solid or liquid.

REGOLITH. A general term for the entire layer or mantle of fragmental and loose, incoherent, or unconsolidated rock material, of whatever origin and of very varied character, that nearly everywhere forms the surface of the land and overlies or covers the more coherent bedrock.

RELATIVE CHRONOLOGY. Geochronology in which the time-order is based on superposition and/or fossil content rather than on an age expressed in years.

RESISTIVITY METHOD. Any electrical exploration method in which current is introduced in the ground by two contact electrodes and potential differences are measured between two or more other electrodes.

RETICLE. A system of wires, cross hairs, threads, dots, or very fine etched lines, placed in the eyepiece of an optical instrument perpendicular to its principal focus.

RHINESTONE. An inexpensive and lustrous imitation of diamond, consisting of glass that has been backed with a thin leaf of metallic foil to simulate the brilliancy of a diamond.

RHYOLITE. A group of extrusive igneous rocks, generally porphyritic and exhibiting flow texture, with phenocrysts of quartz and alkali feldspar in a glassy to cryptocrystalline groundmass.

RILL MARK. A small, dendritic channel, groove, or furrow formed on the surface of beach mud or sand by a wave-generated rill or by a retreating tide.

RIPARIAN. Pertaining to or situated on the bank of a body of water, especially of a watercourse such as a river.

RIPPLE MARK. An undulatory surface or surface sculpture consisting of alternating, subparallel, usually small-scale ridges and hollows of primary origin.

ROCK SALT. Coarsely crystalline halite occurring as a massive, fibrous,
or granular aggregate, and constituting a nearly pure sedimentary
rock that may occur in domes or plugs or as extensive beds resulting from evaporation of saline water.

ROSE QUARTZ. A pink to rose-red and commonly massive variety of
crystalline quartz often used as a gemstone or ornamental stone.

ROSIWAL ANALYSIS. In petrography, a quantitative method of estimating the volume percentages of the minerals in a rock.

RUBY. The red variety of corundum, containing small amounts of
chromium used as a gemstone.

RUTILE. A usually reddish-brown tetragonal mineral: TiO_2.

SALINE SOIL. A nonalkali soil containing sufficient soluble salts to im-
pair its productivity.

SALTATION. A mode of sediment transport in which the particles are
moved progressively forward in a series of short intermittent
leaps, jumps, hops, or bounces from a bottom surface.

SANDSTONE. A medium-grained, clastic sedimentary rock composed of
abundant and rounded or angular fragments of sand size set in a
fine-grained matrix and more or less firmly united by a cementing
material.

SAPROPEL. An unconsolidated, jelly-like ooze or sludge composed of
plant remains, most often algae, macerating and putrifying in an
anaerobic environment on the shallow bottoms of lakes and seas.

SCHIST. A strongly foliated crystalline rock formed by dynamic
metamorphism which can be readily split into thin layers or flakes
due to the well-developed parallelism of more than 50 percent of
the minerals present, particularly those of elongate prismatic
habit.

SEISMIC. Pertaining to an earthquake or Earth vibration, including
those which are artificially induced.

SERPENTINE. A group of common rock-forming minerals having the
formula: $(Mg, Fe)_3Si_2O_5(OH)_4$. They have a greasy or silky luster,
a slightly soapy feel, and a tough, conchoidal fracture.

SHALE. A fine-grained indurated, detrital sedimentary rock formed by
the consolidation of clay, silt, or mud and characterized by finely
stratified structure and/or fissility that is approximately parallel to
the bedding and that is commonly most conspicuous on weathered
surfaces.

SILICA-ALUMINA RATIO. The molecules of silicon dioxide per molecule
of aluminum oxide in clay minerals or in soils.

SILICA-SESQUIOXIDE RATIO. The molecules of silicon dioxide per molecule of aluminum oxide plus ferric oxide in clay minerals or soils.

SILL. A tabular igneous instrusion that parallels the planar structure of the surrounding rock.

SILLIMANITE. A brown, grayish, pale-green, or white orthorhombic mineral: Al_2SiO_5.

SILTSTONE. An indurated or somewhat indurated silt having the texture and composition but lacking the fine lamination or fissility of shale.

SKELETAL. Pertaining to material derived from organisms and consisting of the hard parts secreted by the organisms or of the hard material around or within organic tissue.

SLATE. A compact, fine-grained, metamorphic rock formed from such rocks as shale and volcanic ash, which possesses the property of fissility along planes independent of the original bedding, whereby they can be divided into plates which are lithologically indistinguishable.

SLICKENSIDE. A polished and smoothly striated surface that results from friction along a fault plane.

SMOKY QUARTZ. A smoky-yellow, smoky-brown, or brownish gray and often transparent variety of crystalline quartz sometimes used as a semiprecious gemstone.

SOAPSTONE. A metamorphic rock of massive, schistose or interlaced fibrous texture and soft, unctuous feel composed essentially of talc.

SOIL HORIZON. A layer of soil or soil material approximately parallel to the land surface and differing from adjacent genetically related layers in physical, chemical, and biological properties or characteristics such as color, structure, texture, consistency, kinds and numbers of organisms present, degree of acidity or alkalinity, etc.

SOIL SEPARATES. Mineral particles less than 2.0 mm in equivalent diameter ranging between specified size limits.

SOIL SOLUTION. The aqueous liquid phase of the soil and its solutes consisting of ions dissociated from the surfaces of the soil particles and of other soluble materials.

SOIL STRUCTURE. The combination or arrangement of primary soil particles into secondary particles, units or peds.

SOIL TEXTURE. The relative proportions of the various soil separates in a soil.

SOIL TYPE. The lowest unit in the natural system of soil classification; a subdivision of soil series and consisting of or describing soils that are alike in all characteristics including the texture of the A horizon.

SOIL VARIANT. A soil whose properties are believed to be sufficiently different from other known soils to justify a new series name but comprising such a limited geographic area that creation of a new series is not justified.

SORTING. The dynamic process by which sedimentary particles having some particular characteristic are naturally selected and separated from associated but dissimilar particles by the agents of transportation.

SPHALERITE. A brown or black, sometimes yellow or white, isometric mineral: (Zn, Fe)S. It is a widely distributed ore of zinc.

SPINEL. A mineral: $MgAl_2O_4$ having a great hardness, usually forms octahedral crystals, varies widely in color and is used as a gemstone.

SPIT. A small point or low tongue or narrow embankment of land commonly consisting of sand or gravel deposited by long-shore drifting and having one end attached to the mainland and the other terminating in open water.

STALACTITE. A conical or cylindrical speleothem that is developed and hangs from the roof of a cave. It is deposited by dripping water and is usually composed of calcium carbonate but may also be formed of metallic carbonates.

STALAGMITE. A conical speleothem that is developed upwards from the floor of a cave by the action of dripping water. It is usually composed of calcium carbonate but may be composed of metallic carbonates.

STAUROLITE. A brownish to black orthorhombic mineral: $(Fe, Mg)_2Al_9Si_4O_{23}(OH)$. It is often twined so as to resemble a cross.

STRATIGRAPHY. The branch of geology that deals with the definition and description of major and minor natural divisions of rocks available for study in outcrop or from subsurface and with the interpretation of their significance in geologic history.

STREAK. The color of a mineral in its powdered form, usually obtained by rubbing the mineral on a streak plate and observing the mark it leaves.

STRIATION. A superficial scratch, a tiny furrow, or a thread-like line inscribed on a rock surface or rock fragment by a geologic agent, and usually occurring as one of a series of parallel or subparallel lines.

STRIKE. The direction or trend that a structural surface takes as it intersects the horizontal.

SUNSTONE. An aventurine feldspar.

SYENITE. A group of plutonic rocks containing alkali feldspar, a small amount of plagioclase, one or more mafic minerals and quartz.

TACONITE. A local term used in the Lake Superior iron-bearing district of Minnesota for any bedded ferruginous chert or variously tinted jaspery rock.

TALC. An extremely soft, whitish, greenish or grayish monoclinic mineral: $Mg_3Si_4O_{10}(OH)_2$. It has a characteristic soapy or greasy feel and can be cut with a knife.

TALUS. Rock fragments of any size or shape derived from and lying at the base of a cliff or a very steep, rocky slope.

TERRA-COTTA. A fired or kiln-burnt clay of a peculiar brownish-red or yellowish-red color, used for statuettes, vases, etc., and for ornamental work on the exterior of buildings.

TERRA ROSSA. A reddish-brown, residual soil found as a mantle over limestone bedrock.

TETRAGONAL SYSTEM. One of the six crystal systems. See Figure 3-3.

TIDEWATER. Water that overflows the land during a flood tide.

TILL. Unsorted and unstratified drift, generally unconsolidated deposited directly by and underneath a glacier, without subsequent reworking by water from the glacier.

TOMBOLO. A sand or gravel bar that connects an island with the mainland or another island.

TOPAZ. A white orthorhombic mineral: $Al_2SiO_4(F, OH)_2$. It has a hardness of 8 on Mohs' scale and is used as a gemstone.

TOURMALINE. A group of minerals of general formula: $(Na, Ca)(Mg, Fe^{2+}, Fe^{3+}, Al, Li)_3Al_6(BO_3)_3Si_6O_{18}(OH)_4$. It sometimes contains fluorine in small amounts.

TRACE ELEMENT. An element that is not essential in a mineral but that is found in small quantities in its structure or adsorbed on its surfaces.

TRAVERTINE. A hard, dense, finely crystalline, compact or massive but often concretionary limestone, of white tan or cream color, often having a fibrous or concentric structure and splintery fracture.

TREMOLITE. A white to dark-gray monoclinic mineral of the amphibole group. It has varying amounts of iron, and may contain manganese and chromium.

TRICLINIC. One of the six crystal systems. See Figure 3-3.

TRILOBITE. Any marine arthropod belonging to the class *Trilobita*, characterized by a three-lobed, ovoid to subelliptical exoskeleton divisible into axial and side regions and transversely into anterior, middle, and posterior regions.

TRIPOLI. A finely divided, very porous, lightweight, friable and white, gray, pink, red, buff, or yellow siliceous sedimentary rock occurring confined to the earth's surface usually in powdery or earthy masses and resulting from the weathering of chert or siliceous limestone.

TUFA. A chemical sedimentary rock composed of calcium carbonate, formed by evaporation.

TURBIDITY CURRENT. A density current in water, air, or other fluid caused by different amounts of matter in suspension.

VARVE. A sedimentary bed or lamina or sequence of laminae deposited in a body of still water within one year's time.

VERMICULITE. A group of platy or micaceous clay minerals closely related to chlorite and montmorillonite and having the general formula: $(Mg, Fe, Al)_3(Al, Si)_4O_{10}(OH)_2 \cdot 4H_2O$.

VESICLE. A cavity of variable shape in a lava formed by the entrapment of a gas bubble during solidification of the lava.

WARRANT. A term used in England for a particularly "hard and tough" underclay.

WATERLOGGED. Saturated with water.

WELL LOG. A log obtained from a well, showing such information as resistivity, radioactivity, spontaneous potential and acoustic velocity as a function of depth.

XENOLITH. An inclusion in an igneous rock to which it is not genetically related.

ZEOLITE. A generic term for a large group of white or colorless hydrous aluminosilicates that are analogous in composition to the feldspars, with sodium, calcium, and potassium as their chief metals.

ZIRCON. A mineral: $ZrSiO_4$; a common accessory mineral in siliceous igneous rocks, crystalline, schists and gneisses and in sedimentary rocks derived therefrom and in beach and river placer deposits. An exceptionally brilliant gemstone.

ZONE OF SATURATION. A subsurface zone in which all the interstices are filled with water under pressure greater than that of the atmosphere.

Index